More Praise for *The IEP From A to Z*

"This is a must-own manual for anyone involved in IEP development and special education instruction. It goes far beyond the standard academic goals to address all the 'knottiest' skill deficits that make learning so challenging for students with ADHD, autism spectrum disorders, language disabilities and nonverbal learning disorder. I get asked all the time about how to write IEP goals for this population. I finally have the resource I need. This book not only provides a clear-eyed understanding of the IEP process; it also provides a multitude of concrete examples of IEP goals and objectives as well as nuggets of wisdom regarding teaching strategies. No special education team should be without this book."

—**Peg Dawson**, Ed.D., author, *Smart But Scattered: The Revolutionary "Executive Skills" Approach to Helping Kids Reach Their Potential*

"Finally, a much-needed book to guide parents and teachers through the rigors of creating IEPs. This book offers a blueprint for constructing IEPs that will be useful and not just another exercise. The authors provide us with templates and examples that work in the real world of the classroom. Anyone involved in this process—parents, students, teachers, and other professionals—should have this book on their shelves."

—**John J. Ratey**, M.D., clinical associate professor of psychiatry, Harvard Medical School

"This book will be a practical and invaluable resource for professionals and parents challenged with writing meaningful and functional IEPs for a range of students with developmental challenges."

—**Barry M. Prizant**, Ph.D., CCC-SLP, adjunct professor, Center for the Study of Human Development, Brown University

JOSSEY-BASS TEACHER

Jossey-Bass Teacher provides educators and parents with practical knowledge and tools to create a positive and lifelong impact on student learning. We offer classroom-tested and research-based teaching resources for a variety of grade levels and subject areas. Whether you are a parent, teacher, or another professional working with children in grades K-12, we want to help you make every learning experience successful.

From ready-to-use learning activities to the latest teaching framework, our value-packed books provide insightful, practical, and comprehensive materials on the topics that matter most. We hope to become your trusted source for the best ideas from the most experienced and respected experts in the field.

THE IEP FROM A TO Z

How to Create Meaningful and Measurable Goals and Objectives

DIANE TWACHTMAN-CULLEN

JENNIFER TWACHTMAN-BASSETT

JOSSEY-BASS
A Wiley Imprint
www.josseybass.com

Published by Jossey-Bass
A Wiley Imprint
989 Market Street, San Francisco, CA 94103-1741—www.josseybass.com

Readers should be aware that Internet Web sites offered as citations and/or sources for further information may have changed or disappeared between the time this was written and when it is read.

Limit of Liability/Disclaimer of Warranty: While the publisher and author have used their best efforts in preparing this book, they make no representations or warranties with respect to the accuracy or completeness of the contents of this book and specifically disclaim any implied warranties of merchantability or fitness for a particular purpose. No warranty may be created or extended by sales representatives or written sales materials. The advice and strategies contained herein may not be suitable for your situation. You should consult with a professional where appropriate. Neither the publisher nor author shall be liable for any loss of profit or any other commercial damages, including but not limited to special, incidental, consequential, or other damages.

Jossey-Bass books and products are available through most bookstores. To contact Jossey-Bass directly call our Customer Care Department within the U.S. at 800-956-7739, outside the U.S. at 317-572-3986, or fax 317-572-4002.

Jossey-Bass also publishes its books in a variety of electronic formats. Some content that appears in print may not be available in electronic books.

Library of Congress Cataloging-in-Publication Data
Twachtman-Cullen, Diane.
  The IEP from A to Z : how to create meaningful and measurable objectives / Diane Twachtman-Cullen, Jennifer Twachtman-Bassett. — 2nd ed.
      p. cm.
   Includes bibliographical references and index.
   ISBN 978-0-470-56234-5 (pbk.), 978-1-118-01565-0 (ebk.), 978-1-118-01566-7 (ebk.), 978-1-118-01567-4 (ebk.)
   1. Individualized education programs—United States. 2. Children with disabilities—Education—United States. 3. Educational tests and measurements—United States. I. Twachtman-Bassett, Jennifer. II. Title.
   LC4031.T94 2011
   371.90973—dc22

                                                                        2010051343

FIRST EDITION

PB Printing 10 9 8 7 6 5 4 3 2 1

CONTENTS

PART TWO:
MOVING FROM THEORY TO PRACTICE

Diane Twachtman-Cullen
To my precious grandchildren Alex, Grace, Ali, and Lindsey
You have enriched my life in *every* way imaginable.

Jennifer Twachtman-Bassett
To my precious children Grace and Lindsey
You have taught me that *every* moment counts.

ACKNOWLEDGMENTS

First and foremost, we would like to express our deepest gratitude to the students who inspired this work, and to their families who give eloquent voice to their children's right to a free appropriate public education. For those educators, clinicians, and enlightened administrators who have the best educational interests of their students at heart and will go "the extra mile" even if it means more paperwork, you have our unending admiration and respect. At the very top of that list is Nancy Redmond, Assistant Director of Exceptional Student Education and Student Services for the Volusia County Public Schools in Florida. It was Nancy who said, "The two of you should write a book about the IEP." We are grateful to her for the prompt, the example she has set, and her friendship. Thanks also go to the Volusia County Public Schools and ESE staff for their support of our work, and most particularly for giving us the opportunity to address IEP development for parents and school personnel. We are particularly grateful to Heather Cullen and Sandra Rodrigue for providing the critical resource material that has made such a difference in this book. Special thanks go to Pat Rasch for all of her hard work in the initial stages of this project, and to Paul Collins for his invaluable input regarding children with emotional problems. We also extend our appreciation to Alma Bair, parent extraordinaire, for her very kind comments about the original book and for her excellent suggestions and guidance regarding this one. We are deeply indebted to the wonderful crew at Jossey-Bass/Wiley: to Marjorie McAneny for seeing this project through from A to Z (pun intended!); editorial assistant Tracy Gallagher for all of her hard work; Pamela Berkman for everything she has done to see this project through to completion; Sandra Beris for her excellent copyediting (it can't be easy to edit editors!); and Michael Cook for his exquisite "we loved it the minute we saw it" cover design. We also extend our heartfelt thanks to those all-important people involved in the "end game": Rebecca Still, Dimi Berkner, Hunter Stark, Sophia Ho, and Cheryl Duksta. Finally, we extend our deepest appreciation to Peter W. D. Wright, Esquire, for his superb foreword. We are humbled to have the imprimatur of a man who has been at the very center of special education law in this country, and one who has done so much to help students receive appropriate education that is individualized to their needs.

Diane Twachtman-Cullen, Ph.D., CCC-SLP
Jennifer Twachtman-Bassett, M.S., CCC-SLP

THE AUTHORS

Diane Twachtman-Cullen, Ph.D., CCC-SLP, is a licensed speech-language pathologist specializing in autism spectrum conditions and related disorders. She is the author of numerous chapters and articles, as well as three books: *A Passion to Believe: Autism and the Facilitated Communication Phenomenon*; *Trevor Trevor,* a metaphor for children designed to increase the sensitivity of typical peers toward their classmates with special needs; and *How to Be a Para Pro: A Comprehensive Training Manual for Paraprofessionals.* Dr. Twachtman-Cullen is the editor-in-chief of *Autism Spectrum Quarterly* (www.ASQuarterly.com), a MAGAJOURNAL® that bridges the gap between the research and general autism communities. A member and past co-chairperson of the Panel of Professional Advisors of the Autism Society of America, Dr. Twachtman-Cullen serves on several other professional advisory boards and was a member of the National Behavioral Health Quality Advisory Committee for the Aetna Insurance Company. She is also the recipient of the 2006 Divine Neurotypical Award (DNA) given by the Global and Regional Asperger Syndrome Partnership, Inc. (GRASP) to an individual who has made a significant contribution to the lives of those with autism and Asperger syndrome. Dr. Twachtman-Cullen provides consultative services and training seminars internationally on a variety of topics, and participated as an invited delegate in the Shafallah Center Forum in Doha, Qatar, in 2007 and 2008. She was also an invited delegate to, and speaker at, the first-ever professional conference sponsored by the United Kingdom–based National Autistic Society, held in Manchester, England, in March 2010. Dr. Twachtman-Cullen currently serves as a panel member of and consultant to the Imperative Pictures Group in Hollywood, California. Her consultation agency, ADDCON Center, LLC is located in Higganum, Connecticut (addconcenter@snet.net).

Jennifer Twachtman-Bassett, M.S., CCC-SLP, is a speech-language pathologist and member of the Autism Society of America's Panel of Professional Advisors. She also serves on the board of directors of the Autism Society of Connecticut. Ms. Twachtman-Bassett is part of the Autism Spectrum Assessment Program at Connecticut Children's Medical Center (CCMC) where, in collaboration with the Department of Developmental Pediatrics, she is involved in the diagnosis of children with autism spectrum disorders. Ms. Twachtman-Bassett also provides social language and problem-solving evaluations for older children with Asperger syndrome and related conditions, as well as individual therapy and parent training. She has also served on CCMC's Clinical Feeding Team. In addition, Ms. Twachtman-Bassett is the speech-language consultant at Butler Hospital in Providence, Rhode Island, where she conducts evaluations and provides strategies for addressing social and language-based aspects of problem solving and behavioral issues. She has spent many years working in both public and private special education school settings with children with autism and related disabilities, and has been a full participant in the IEP process. Ms. Twachtman-Bassett is the associate editor of *Autism Spectrum Quarterly,* where she also contributes a column on translating research into practice. She has written several articles and chapters on issues related to communication, language, and feeding issues in autism spectrum conditions, and has also presented workshops at state, regional, and national conferences.

AUTHORS' NOTE

This book is written from an educational, not a legal, perspective, and is based on our interpretation of special education law IDEA 2004 as it relates to IEP development. We acknowledge that interpretation of some aspects of the law may differ from state to state, and from school district to school district. Ours relies heavily on our opinion of what is in the best educational interests of students with special needs. This book is in no way intended to advise readers on matters of law, or to serve as a substitute for obtaining sound legal advice from qualified professionals where it is warranted or desired. References and citations to the law are rendered purely for informational purposes, and as a context for our opinions.

FOREWORD

As an attorney who has represented children with special educational needs, received a unanimous decision from the United States Supreme Court, coauthored the *Wrightslaw* special education law and advocacy books, cofounded the Wrightslaw.com website, and taught as an adjunct law professor, I have seen thousands of Individualized Education Programs (IEPs) and have read many books on the topic. As a person who has dyslexia and ADHD, being asked to write the Foreword for this book about IEPs is an honor.

In 2002, Diane Twachtman-Cullen and her daughter, Jennifer Twachtman-Bassett, coauthored *How Well Does Your IEP Measure Up?* In my review of that best-selling book I wrote, "Finally, an IEP book that focuses on the 'science' of writing clear, understandable, and measurable objectives. The authors brilliantly expose the absurdity of public school IEPs and their bizarre, fuzzy-wuzzy language."

When I was asked to write this Foreword, I struggled with how to express the fact that the authors did an even better job with this book. This is more than a second edition to the earlier work. Although *The IEP from A to Z: How to Create Meaningful and Measurable Goals and Objectives* covers some of the same material, it is far more comprehensive.

Too often, IEPs contain meaningless goals that are useless to teachers and parents. In this book, the authors provide a framework for writing goals and short-term objectives so that they mesh with popular progress reporting schedules, such as three short-term objectives and one annual goal.

When educators and parents look for IEP goals and objectives that are specific to a particular disability, they fall into the trap of "pigeonholing" the child with a label, and fail to focus on the child's unique educational needs. This book describes diverse deficits that occur in children with many different disabilities, without regard to "labels." These deficits affect executive function skills, concept development, language comprehension and expression, narrative development, social cognition, critical thinking, and more.

At the same time, the parent and educator who need to address educational issues in autism spectrum disorders, attention deficit disorders, speech and language disabilities, nonverbal learning disorder, and emotional and behavioral disorders, will find the templates for goals and objectives invaluable.

In crafting an IEP, how does a teacher or parent quantify, in an objective observable manner through data collection, something that seems impossible to quantify or describe in a goal or objective? How does a teacher or parent address the acquisition of social and behavioral skills, executive function skills, and functional performance? These areas are problematic in most IEPs. Acknowledging this, Diane and Jennifer not only focus on how to write appropriate goals and objectives but also resolve these problems with clear how-to examples.

I urge you to read this book three times. On your first read, go through the book, from cover to cover. Do not use a pen or highlighter. On the second read, the essential concepts will fall into place. Make margin notes and highlight key areas. On your third read, go back and review your notes and highlighted areas.

After you finish the third read, your approach to the next IEP, whether for one of your students or your own child, will be a new experience. As you identify the truly important goals and objectives and put pen to paper, you will feel confident that, as the authors stress throughout the book, you are helping the child acquire the skills necessary to lead a productive, independent life.

This book should be required reading for every special educator and every parent of a child with special educational needs.

Peter W. D. Wright
Attorney at Law
Publisher, Wrightslaw.com
Deltaville, Virginia

THE IEP FROM
A TO Z

A journey of a thousand miles begins with the first step.

—*Chinese proverb*

INTRODUCTION

It is said that you can't judge a book by its cover. You can, however, tell a great deal about the philosophy and content of this book from its title. In the case of *The IEP from A to Z: How to Create Meaningful and Measurable Goals and Objectives,* our intent is to be both thorough and comprehensive in addressing the essential elements of the IEP; the relevant changes to the reauthorized Individuals with Disabilities Education Improvement Act of 2004 (IDEA 2004); and the ramifications of these changes for students with special needs. It is our goal then to provide IEP teams with critical information about the essential elements that go into IEP development, as well as to present specific examples of how to apply these elements in practice so that they reflect the new focus on accountability and improved outcomes in IDEA 2004.

Unfortunately, in our increasingly litigious society, holding the IEP to any standard is enough to conjure up images of due process hearings. Although we recognize that in some instances due process may be necessary when IEPs don't pass muster, we leave the task of directing parents through that arduous procedure to other writers with legal expertise. In fact, we advocate avoiding due process whenever possible. Toward this end, we offer readers a modus operandi for doing just that—a step-by-step guide to help parents, educators, clinicians, and special education supervisors to get the right education program in place at the outset, thereby avoiding the need for future legal action. Simply stated, this book is about how to write thoughtful, intelligent IEPs that deliver high-quality, need-based educational programming to students with autism spectrum disorders (ASD);

speech or language impairment (S/LI), including disorders of communication; nonverbal learning disability (NLD); attention deficit disorder/attention deficit hyperactivity disorder (ADD/ADHD); and emotional disturbance (ED).

When an earlier version of this book was originally published in 2002, it reflected changes to the special education law that were made in the 1990s. The current volume has been updated to reflect the most current revisions to the law as they pertain to IEP development. We have also expanded the book's focus from that of the single disability category of *autism spectrum disorders* (ASD) to include all the disability categories listed in the preceding paragraph. We had two reasons for doing this. First, there are many overlapping educational needs in the areas of cognitive and social-cognitive functioning and communication and language use among students with these conditions. Second, these conditions share a kind of invisibility that can keep the needs of these students under the radar. In other words, many students with ASD, S/LI, NLD, ADD/ADHD, and ED don't present with obvious signs of disability but rather with certain behaviors that, when held to a standard appropriate to typically developing individuals, place them in an unfavorable light. This is because the symptoms associated with these conditions are not always recognized as reflections of compromises in neurological or cognitive functioning, but rather as behaviors over which the student has control. The overarching consequence of misjudging a student's behavior as willful or volitional, or as reflecting a lack of motivation or laziness, is that the child's educational needs go unmet. It is our hope that, by shedding light on the sometimes subtle deficits with which these students present, we will encourage IEP teams to recognize the need to provide instructional support and accommodations for these students, while at the same time discourage them from characterizing the students' deficits as "behavioral" in nature. It is well beyond the scope of this book to provide detailed information on each of the disability categories covered, but there are many excellent resources for this purpose listed in Appendix B. Readers are also encouraged to seek out additional information on their own.

The underlying premise of this book is that the IEP is the individualized "blueprint" that delineates appropriate educational programming. As such, like other blueprints, it must contain the exact specifications and conditions necessary to guide the "builders" of education programs. The organization of the book reflects this premise. After a brief but instructive historical overview of special education law in Chapter One, the remaining chapters in Part One of the book contain the following "building specs" that make up the essential elements of IEP development: present levels of performance (PLPs); underlying conditions governing performance; methodology; criteria and prompt levels; generalization; annual goals, short-term objectives and benchmarks; evaluation and data collection; and an IEP potpourri consisting of information related to least restrictive environment (LRE), state or districtwide assessments, accommodations and modifications, related services, and supplementary aids and services. Our goal in Part One is to provide the specific information needed—the building specs—to generate the types of meaningful annual goals, short-term objectives, or benchmarks that lead to effective service delivery.

Part Two of the book presents several "builder's models," if you will, to help readers see how the information outlined in Part One leads to comprehensive, clearly defined IEP annual goals and short-term objectives for the various disability categories. Chapter Ten discusses assessment considerations, particularly as they relate to determining priority educational needs. It also serves as the introduction to Part Two. Chapters Eleven through Fourteen contain sample PLPs, annual goals, and short-term objectives related to the following areas of cognitive and social-cognitive functioning: communication, language, and speech; nonverbal comprehension and expression; social relatedness and interaction, play, and leisure skills; executive function; theory of mind; and critical thinking. In addition, we provide the reader with recommended educational programming formats, general teaching tips and strategies, and teaching resources, all of which are designed to help IEP teams translate goals and objectives into sound educational practices. There is also an epilogue, intended to provide a cohesive, concluding statement on the crucial link between well-stated IEP goals and objectives and effective service delivery.

Our goal in Part Two is to put it all together, so that the reader can see, from the many examples given, exactly how the various elements of the IEP can lead to a whole far greater than the sum of its individual parts—that is, the delivery of an appropriate, individualized education program. The importance of including practical information on programming formats, teaching strategies, and resource materials cannot be overstated, particularly because students with these conditions require highly specialized programming beyond that commonly found in what may be called standard special education fare. We take our lead from students with ASD for whom "traditional special education programs" leave much to be desired (Peeters and Gillberg, 1999, p. 79). In fact, Peeters and Gillberg candidly state that "special education which offers the type of teaching used in mental retardation (which consists principally of simplification) does not suffice" (p. 79). We believe that this is also true for students with the conditions covered in this book.

The book's user-friendly features include pull quotes, bulleted lists, case studies, and chapter summaries, all intended to make information both easily accessible and readily usable. Finally, *The IEP from A to Z* is intended for *anyone*—parent or professional—whose ultimate goal is to write high-quality IEPs for students with ASD, S/LI, NLD, ADD/ADHD, and ED that meet both the letter and spirit of the law and that lead to the delivery of effective educational services and outcomes. If there is a bias it is in the student's favor, for in all issues discussed in this book we operated from the perspective of what is in the best educational interests of the student. Our greatest wish is that the information we offer here will enable parents and school personnel to work together, as equal partners, to build educational programs of value for students with special needs.

Diane Twachtman-Cullen, Ph.D., CCC-SLP
Jennifer Twachtman-Bassett, M.S., CCC-SLP

Essential Elements of the IEP

CHAPTER

1

PAST PERSPECTIVES AND PRESENT PRACTICES

"The farther backward you look, the farther forward you can see."

—*Winston Churchill*

More than thirty-five years have passed since the event that revolutionized the face of special education services in the United States: the 1975 enactment of *Public Law 94–142*, the *Education for All Handicapped Children Act (EHA)*. This landmark legislation gave birth to two critically important interrelated concepts. The first was that of a *free appropriate public education (FAPE)*—the legal standard-bearer for educational programming for students with disabilities. The second was that of the *individualized education plan (IEP)*, the multifaceted document designed both to benefit and to protect children with special needs and to provide their parents with procedural safeguards.

Having come into existence in the era when management by objectives and accountability were the catch phrases of the day, the IEP offered the promise of welcome relief from nebulous, catch-as-catch-can instruction. It also offered a systematic approach to educational programming by requiring that educational goals and objectives not only be stated in outcome-based behavioral terms but also that they be measurable. Hence, the IEP also emphasized the importance of data collection for the purpose of determining how well educational programming was meeting the needs of students with disabilities.

A NEW DECADE, NEW CHANGES

If P.L. 94–142 offered a foot in the door marked by FAPE, its next incarnation pushed that door wide open. The year was 1990. The event was the reauthorization of P.L. 94–142 under the new title *Individuals with Disabilities Education Act (IDEA)*. This law not only reaffirmed the importance of individualized education for students with disabilities but also granted official status to *autism* as an individual disability category under the law. For the first time, students with autism were able to receive educational services under the category label that most accurately reflected their disability. The inclusion of autism as a separate category was heralded by parents and professionals alike, for it underscored the enigmatic nature of the condition and the unique educational challenges faced by students with the condition.

The IEP offered a systematic approach to educational programming by requiring that educational goals and objectives not only be stated in outcome-based behavioral terms but also that they be measurable.

The 1990s were a fertile decade for special education law. Nine years after the reauthorization of P.L. 94–142 as IDEA, new amendments gave the law even greater clout. One of the most significant contributions of the new amendments was an emphasis on staff training, an issue uppermost in the minds of parents. In fact, states were held to a higher standard than previously, "whereby they [had to] *ensure* that those who provided services for students with disabilities (professionals and paraprofessionals alike) had an adequate knowledge base and the skills" (Twachtman-Cullen, 2000a, p. ix) necessary to meet the needs of these students. The inclusion of paraprofessionals in the training loop was a great victory for parents, many of whom had complained bitterly—and in our opinion, rightfully—that the person closest to their child (the paraprofessional) was the one with the least amount of knowledge and training.

On the surface it appeared that "everything was coming up roses" for students with disabilities and their parents. After all, the list of requirements for schools under IDEA read like a parents' wish list: *related services; supplementary aids and services; assistive technology support; transition*; and the specification of necessary *accommodations or modifications*. Beneath the surface, however, the picture wasn't quite so rosy.

For one thing, for many parents the IEP process was frightening and intimidating, and in many cases more often hierarchical than collaborative. This was because parents weren't always granted the equal-partner status that the law afforded them. For another, parents and educators often found themselves at odds on important issues. This was particularly apparent when it came to their views on the standard of *appropriateness*, because the law itself was essentially silent on its interpretation. Typically, schools looked on appropriateness as a *minimal* court-sanctioned standard—the so-called *Chevrolet*. Parents, however, found the school's minimalist position unacceptable, preferring instead that schools *maximize* their children's education by providing the *Cadillac* instead of the Chevy. Little did anyone know at the time that the appropriateness standard would soon take on a whole new meaning.

A NEW CENTURY, NEW CHANGES, AND A NEW NAME

In December 2004 IDEA was again reauthorized and amended. Now known as the *Individuals with Disabilities Education Improvement Act of 2004* (*IDEA 2004*), its net effect was to raise the bar on what constituted a free appropriate public education (FAPE). As a result, there is a new emphasis (in the Findings section of the law) on high expectations, and an increased focus on accountability—for example, the use of research-based instruction—and improved outcomes, such as further education, all of which are designed to bring "IDEA 2004 into conformity with the No Child Left Behind Act (NCLB)" (Wright and Wright, 2006, p. 19). In service to this goal, many of the definitions seen in IDEA 2004 come directly from NCLB. For example, section 1412 (a) (15) of IDEA 2004 applies the *adequate yearly progress* standard from NCLB to children with disabilities. Indeed, the influence of NCLB was so great that IDEA 2004 also placed greater emphasis on academic subjects such as reading and on early intervention (Wright and Wright, 2006). Moreover, where the earlier versions of IDEA were focused on more global—even generic—concerns, such as access to FAPE and procedural safeguards, the latest revision is clearly more concerned with specific refinements to the law and an elevation of standards. Consider the way in which the phrase *to the maximum extent possible* has changed in IDEA 2004. Where the phrase used to refer to *access* to the general curriculum, today it goes far beyond mere access by requiring educators not only to meet developmental goals but also to meet "to the *maximum extent possible* [italics added], the challenging expectations that have been established for all children" (Wright and Wright, 2006, p. 46). Clearly, the new language in IDEA 2004 reflects the profound and intended influence of NCLB. Indeed, according to Steedman (Summer, 2005): "IDEA 2004 requires that states establish performance goals for children with disabilities that are the same as the state's definition of adequate yearly progress under NCLB" (p. 34). Furthermore, IDEA 2004 also follows the lead of NCLB by requiring "highly qualified special education teachers" (Wright and Wright, 2006, p. 19). Hence, there is a very important interface between IDEA 2004 and NCLB that has the effect of holding children with disabilities and special education teachers to higher standards that are more comparable to those that apply to nondisabled students and general education teachers.

In keeping with the focus on higher standards, IDEA 2004 also raised the bar on methodology by requiring that instructional practices, related services, and supplementary aids and services all be based on peer-reviewed research. The decision about whether to include instructional methodology in the IEP rests with the IEP team; however, the new evidence-based standard clearly ups the ante in favor of its inclusion in the document. Methodology issues will be discussed more fully in Chapter Four.

Undoubtedly the greatest change in IDEA 2004—and the most controversial—is the elimination of short-term objectives and benchmarks for all students except those who receive alternate assessments. This change was made, ostensibly, to save time and reduce the amount of paperwork for educators. Unfortunately, it may do neither. Because the annual goals for students are still required to be both specific and measurable, eliminating objectives and benchmarks for those students who are assessed (under NCLB) via grade-level standards may actually make the process of determining progress toward the goal more arduous. It removes the logical, incremental framework—the short-term objectives or benchmarks—within which to gauge progress and make midcourse corrections. It is our opinion that the decision to eliminate objectives and benchmarks for what may amount to the majority of special needs students was shortsighted at best and inimical to the needs of these students at worst. Hence, we strongly advise IEP teams to continue to apply one or the other progress indicator as the means by which to determine the student's progress toward the annual goals, a practice we will follow in this book and an issue we will revisit many times in Part One of this book.

Another (unwelcome) change under IDEA 2004 concerns multiyear IEPs. Fortunately, because this is a demonstration project that involves no more than fifteen states, it will affect only individuals who reside in those states. Importantly, those individuals should be aware that three-year IEPs require parental consent.

Clearly, this provision, like the one regarding the elimination of objectives and benchmarks, is tied to administrative convenience and is not, in our opinion, in the best interests of students. Hence, we are not in favor of three-year IEPs unless they come equipped with crystal balls!

IDEA 2004 REQUIREMENTS

Although we applaud the trend toward higher expectations for students with disabilities in IDEA 2004, and the move toward a higher standard for judging the appropriateness of educational programming and student progress, we fear that some of the new requirements may actually be inappropriate for many students with special needs. It is our contention that the comingling of IDEA 2004 and NCLB—especially regarding the requirement that children with disabilities meet the standard of *adequate yearly progress* set forth by NCLB—holds these children to a standard that, for some, may be highly unrealistic. For example, Steedman (Summer, 2005), in discussing the NCLB goal of narrowing the gap between children with disabilities and their typically developing peers, states: "If a disabled child is already several academic years behind his nondisabled peers, the only way to 'narrow the gap' is for the disabled child to make more than one year's academic growth in the span of one year" (p. 34). Obviously, this requires the child with a disability to accomplish significantly *more* academically in a year than a nondisabled peer—a standard that is highly unrealistic, and more arbitrary and generic, than individualized to the specific needs of the student.

We are also concerned about the NCLB-like emphasis on academics, particularly given the cognitive and social-cognitive needs of students with ASD, ADD/ADHD, NLD, S/LI, and ED. Many students with these conditions have significant pragmatic communication, language, executive function, and theory of mind deficits, as well as impairments in critical thinking such as problem solving and making inferences. All of these areas of functioning are even more tied to "leading productive and independent lives" (the standard set forth in IDEA 2004) after secondary school than academics per se. Indeed, many students with

> *Although we applaud the trend toward higher expectations for students with disabilities in IDEA 2004 . . . we fear that some of the new requirements may actually be inappropriate for many students with special needs.*

these conditions may do quite well academically even though they do not have the skills in the above-noted critical areas of functioning to enable them to be productive and to function independently in the community. For this reason, our focus in this book is not on academics but rather on such skills that fall under the umbrella of communication, language, and to a lesser extent speech; comprehension and expression of nonverbal cues and signals; social relatedness; executive function; theory of mind; and critical thinking. So important are the skills that fall under this umbrella to independent functioning for students with ASD, ADD/ADHD, NLD, S/LI, and ED that we consider them to be the higher-order life skills that are necessary to enable these students to lead productive and independent lives as set forth in IDEA 2004.

Before we proceed to the next chapter, it is important to note that IDEA 2004 did not make any actual changes to the concept of _least restrictive environment_ (_LRE_). That said, although there is a great deal of variability from state to state and school district to school district when it comes to their philosophies on inclusion, it seems to us that the changes in IDEA 2004 that have been influenced by NCLB have created an even greater emphasis—even if implied—on inclusion than before. So although it is still true that the individual needs of the student should trump the law's long-standing preference for inclusion, this is not always the case in practice. For example, schools in a growing number of states hold students with special needs in inclusive settings to the same types of curricular activities that are appropriate for their peers, even though they are performing well below academic standards and would likely be better served by different programming. In addition, as noted earlier, students with disabilities are also held to the same standard of adequate yearly progress. We believe that these practices give greater weight to inclusive settings vis-à-vis the LRE provision, even though the language regarding LRE has not changed in IDEA 2004. This issue will be addressed more fully in Chapter Nine.

WRAPPING UP THE MAIN POINTS

- The Education for All Handicapped Children Act (EHA) of 1975 gave birth to two critically important concepts: a free appropriate public education (FAPE) for students with disabilities and the individualized education plan (IEP).

- In 2004 IDEA was reauthorized and amended. The net effect of IDEA 2004 was to raise the bar on what constitutes a FAPE.

- The greatest change in IDEA 2004—and the most controversial—is the elimination of short-term objectives and benchmarks for all students except those who receive alternate assessments.

- Comingling of IDEA 2004 and NCLB—especially regarding the requirement that children with disabilities meet the standard of adequate yearly progress set forth by NCLB—holds these children to a standard that may be highly unrealistic.

CHAPTER

2

THE "GOLD STANDARD" FOR SETTING GOALS AND MEASURING PROGRESS

"Without a standard there is no logical basis for making a decision or taking action."

—Joseph M. Juran

IDEA 2004 contains new, more specific language that clearly ties the present levels of performance (PLP) to achievement in traditional academic areas such as reading, math, history, language arts, and the like for students who come under the grade-level performance category. In addition, it also uses the term *functional performance* to refer to those areas that are outside academics.

When one thinks of the term *functional,* the traditional activities of daily living usually come to mind. This would, of course, apply to students for whom grade-level academic performance is not expected—such as those who come under the alternate assessment provision of IDEA 2004. That said, readers are cautioned not to apply the terms *academic* and *functional* in a strict either-or sense because both may be appropriate for some students. To clarify, although it is true that for some significantly challenged students functional performance may be the most appropriate standard for judging progress, for others who are less challenged (but still under the alternate assessment provision) there may also be rudimentary academic goals. In addition, many students with ASD, ADD/ADHD, NLD, S/LI, and ED are able to meet grade-level standards even as they manifest specific cognitive and social-cognitive problems that impede their ability to function adequately or independently in social settings. Hence, for our purposes, we apply the term *functional performance* to students who require goals for many of the nonacademic areas of functioning covered even as we acknowledge that many of these same students may still be able to meet grade-level standards in academic areas. Nonacademic skill areas include pragmatic communication, language, and speech; nonverbal cues and signals; executive function; theory of mind; social relatedness; play/leisure; and critical thinking (for example, making inferences, problem solving, and so on).

IDEA 2004 contains more specific language that clearly ties the PLP to achievement in traditional academic areas and uses the term functional performance *to refer to areas outside academics.*

Apart from the addition of the words *present levels of academic achievement and functional performance*, the requirements for the PLP statement did not change in IDEA 2004. IEP teams must still include information on "[h]ow the child's disability affects the child's involvement and progress in the general education curriculum (i.e., the same curriculum as for nondisabled children); or [f]or preschool children, as appropriate, how the disability affects the child's participation in appropriate activities" (Wright and Wright, 2006, p. 245). The importance of the PLP in the IEP cannot be overstated because (a) it forms the basis for generating annual goals and short-term objectives or benchmarks that are specifically individualized to the student's needs; and (b) it serves as the standard against which to measure performance or progress.

Ironically, the PLP statement is one of the most misunderstood elements of the IEP, and one that is very often neglected. For example, the following "PLPs" are taken directly from an IEP document for an elementary school student with autism:

Social-Emotional/Behavioral: *Has difficulty in this area.*

Communication: *Has made progress.*

The first thing that needs to be said about these statements is that neither one addresses the student's academic achievement or functional performance—that is, what can he or she actually do? Second, neither statement addresses the impact of the student's disability on involvement and progress in the general curriculum, as required by IDEA 2004. Third, both statements are so vague as to be useless with respect to both the judgment of progress and the provision of information necessary to generate individualized goals and objectives.

Sometimes school districts list test scores as the "statement" of present levels of performance. Although this can be appropriate, given the emphasis on academic performance in IDEA 2004, the use of a score as a PLP must be specific enough to serve as an appropriate standard by which to determine progress. Consider the differences in the following two PLP statements, both of which relate to functioning on tests. First:

> *Sara is an eight-year old student who scores at the six-year-old age level on the Peabody Picture Vocabulary Test. This is significantly below her grade-level peers, making it difficult for her to follow directions in class.*

This PLP is tied to performance; leads one to write an annual goal and objectives designed to improve Sara's receptive language ability; and includes a statement regarding how Sara's performance impacts her involvement and progress in the general education curriculum.

Now consider this:

> *Academic/Cognitive: WISC III—V 128 P 111; FS 122*

Unlike the information given for Sara, the information in this PLP is too global to serve as an appropriate standard against which to measure progress. In addition, there is no indication of level of performance in specific areas of functioning; nor is there any statement about the student's involvement and progress in the general education curriculum. Last but not least, the IEP team would be hard-pressed to come up with an annual goal and objectives because there is not enough information given on which to base them.

Test scores need to be relevant to the specific area of functioning under consideration; specific enough to lead to appropriate annual goals and short-term objectives; and capable of serving as the standard against which to measure progress.

The general rule to follow on the use of test scores to document the student's PLP is this: they need to be relevant to the specific area of functioning under consideration; specific enough to lead to appropriate annual goals and short-term objectives; and capable of serving as the standard against which to measure progress.

THE PLP STATEMENT UNDER IDEA 2004

In order for the statement on the student's PLP to be used as the law intended—that is, as the basis for generating goals and objectives, and as the standard by which to determine progress—it needs to meet certain conditions:

- It should be performance-based vis-à-vis the area or domains for which the goals and objectives will be written.

- It should contain a statement explaining how the student's disability affects his or her involvement and progress in the general curriculum (or for preschool children, how it affects their involvement in appropriate activities).

- It should serve as the standard for judging progress.

Furthermore, it's good practice to also include the sources on which the information is based, such as the name of the test if reporting test scores. Let's take a closer look at some of these components.

Present Academic or Functional Performance

The focus here is on current functioning: What is the student able to do or not do vis-à-vis a specific area of functioning? Needless to say, in order for the PLP to serve as the basis for generating annual goals and short-term objectives, as well as the standard for determining progress, it needs to be sufficiently comprehensive. It does not, however, have to be overly long. The following PLP for academic development is far too global to be meaningful, and thus falls far short of the mark on both counts:

Student has moderate academic deficits that adversely affect his educational performance.

It should be noted that in the IEP from which this PLP was taken, academic development was the umbrella category for the subject areas of reading, social studies, math, and science. Clearly, this is an inappropriate PLP because it meets none of the criteria listed in the preceding section. Hence, it would neither lead to the generation of an appropriate annual goal nor serve as an appropriate standard by which to determine progress.

Another common error in writing PLPs is a failure to adequately link them to the goals and objectives written to address them. This would seem obvious, but the following example from a student's IEP clearly reveals an all-too-common lack of synchrony:

> Present level of performance: *Student continues to need verbal and gestural support to move through a conflict or change his expectations.*
>
> Annual goal: *Student will increase his pro-social behavior.*
>
> Short-term objective: *Student will be comfortable in simple social situations (for example, lunch at school).*

Clearly, neither the goal nor the objective follows from the PLP, even though the PLP is the standard for determining progress. (Although we are not addressing goals or objectives in this chapter, we can't ignore the fact that those listed above not only are too vague to be understood but are also not measurable!)

Sometimes the IEP form itself constrains the process of generating appropriate PLPs. In some cases, the amount of space allotted to this essential IEP element is minimal, thus severely limiting the amount of information that can be given. In other cases, forms call for a lengthy narrative. If carefully written, this can meet the previously stated criteria. More often than not, however, PLPs constructed in this manner are rambling narratives that contain irrelevant and outdated information. A far better practice for generating appropriate PLPs is to provide separate descriptions for each of the annual goals, because they would relate more directly to the particular area or domain for which the goals and objectives are to be written. For example, when writing PLPs for academics, we recommend writing individual descriptions for each of the subjects to be addressed (that is, reading, social studies, math, and science), rather than writing one global PLP for academic development.

To serve as the basis for generating annual goals and short-term objectives, as well as the standard for determining progress, the PLP needs to be sufficiently comprehensive.

Involvement and Progress in the General Curriculum

This component of the PLP addresses the impact of the student's disability on his or her ability to be involved and make progress in the general education curriculum. By requiring thoughtful consideration of this issue, IDEA 2004 underscores the importance of the least restrictive environment (LRE) even for students who receive programming in specialized settings, and it also emphasizes the importance of the tie-in to the general curriculum for students with disabilities. Independence, prompt levels, and the need for assistance are appropriately stated here. Moreover, information on these issues provides the basis for determining not only whether accommodations and supports are needed but also the specific types that may be necessary. Despite the importance of these issues, impact statements on involvement and progress in the general curriculum, or in appropriate activities for preschool children, are often sadly lacking in many of today's IEPs. To avoid this, it is recommended that the concluding statement of the PLP directly address the impact of the student's disability on his or her ability to function in the mainstream. This need not be anything more complex than the following:

> Sabrina's executive function deficits impact her ability to function in mainstream educational settings that are not highly structured, or that do not regularly employ visual supports to accompany auditory information.

Sources of Information

Information for the PLP can and should be based on a variety of sources, ranging from formal (when possible) and informal assessments, teacher-clinician observation, student performance data, and parental input. Attribution of the source, although optional, is recommended, because blanket statements made without attribution hold no one accountable for the judgments or observations rendered. In contrast, statements beginning with words such as *reportedly, based upon*, or *according to* not only link judgments to their sources but also go a long way toward embedding them in an appropriate context. The following PLP on executive functioning in a seventh-grade boy with ASD takes into account all of the information in this chapter:

> While John is able to manage his time and personal belongings with the use of visual supports (for example, timers and checklists), he is resistant to using them. Several of his teachers note, however, that without them, he functions less competently. As a result of his disability, John has difficulty keeping up with his mainstream classmates without the use of supports for his executive function deficits.

WRAPPING UP THE MAIN POINTS

- The PLP statement is one of the most misunderstood elements of the IEP and one that is very often neglected.

- The PLP statement should be performance-based and explain how the student's disability affects his or her involvement and progress in the general curriculum.

- When the PLP for a particular domain is both well-stated and comprehensive it not only leads the IEP team down the right path in the generation of annual goals and short-term objectives but also provides a suitable standard against which to measure student performance and progress.

CHAPTER

3

SETUPS FOR SUCCESSFUL PERFORMANCE

"Set yourself up for success and anything is possible."

—*Anonymous*

Performance never occurs in a vacuum. Whether the achievement is a climb to the top of Mount Everest or the safe completion of a tugboat trip, there are unstated but important factors that govern success. In other words, performance is always contingent on certain conditions, whether or not they are explicitly stated.

Exactly what is it that makes performance conditional? In the Mount Everest example, performance is tempered by many things, including both the needs of the climber in the rarefied atmosphere at the top of the mountain and the weather conditions. Without the proper conditions (oxygen supply and adequate weather), performance (climbing to the top of Mount Everest) would not be possible. Likewise, in the tugboat example, safe passage depends on several factors, ranging from the ability of the pilot to the integrity of the tugboat and suitability of weather conditions. Goals for these two activities might be stated, respectively, as follows:

Given a supply of oxygen and adequate weather conditions, Mr. Smith will climb to the top of Mount Everest.

Given appropriate pilot training, a mechanically sound vessel, and adequate weather conditions, Captain Doe will navigate safely from point A to point B.

UNDERLYING CONDITIONS AND PERFORMANCE

These examples illustrate two important points about underlying conditions. First, they can either make or break performance. Therefore, they are powerful contributors to—or if inappropriate—detractors from successful performance. Second, the underlying conditions affect what the performer needs in order to accomplish the task. Simply stated, performance that is eminently possible under appropriate (supportive) conditions may be severely compromised or completely lacking in the absence of those conditions. At the risk of stating the obvious, student success, or the lack thereof, is very much a function of the underlying conditions.

The underlying conditions for the types of activities noted in the preceding examples are so obvious that they really can go without saying and still be addressed. In contrast, it is critical to specify the underlying conditions governing performance for students with the types of conditions covered in this book because of their unique needs for certain types of support in order to achieve success. In fact, we consider the statement of underlying conditions in the IEP to be essential not only to providing successful programming but also to avoiding inappropriate programming.

Consider the following goal written for a preschool child with ADHD who, despite repeated reminders to raise his hand, continues to interrupt the teacher constantly in morning circle:

Jimmy will raise his hand 9/10 times (that is, nine out of ten times, or at the 90% level of performance) when he has something to say in morning circle.

The lack of an underlying condition for performance leaves much to be desired (probably even the successful accomplishment of the objective!). Specifically, if the teacher uses only verbal reminders, chances are that both she and Jimmy will experience a good deal of frustration, albeit for vastly different reasons. When executive skills are weak, as they are in ADHD, verbal reminders alone are insufficient to mediate control of impulsivity. With the appropriate underlying condition, however, the objective is eminently achievable. Consider the following:

Given a picture cue of a child raising his hand, Jimmy will raise his hand 9/10 times when he has something to say in morning circle.

The addition of the underlying condition—the picture of the child raising his hand—gives the student a stable and meaningful cue—an executive function prop, if you will—to remind him of the need to raise his hand. Moreover, it not only gives anyone working on the objective a clear idea of the type of support needed to enable performance but also ensures consistency in the manner in which the objective is addressed across different staff members.

AN UNDERLYING CONDITION AND GOAL FOR TEACHERS AND CLINICIANS

Of course, providing support to compensate for Jimmy's impaired executive function (EF) system in the form of a stable visual cue implies (a) knowing that the student with ADHD has EF difficulty, and (b) knowing that his performance is contingent on this type of visual support. Although most educators are aware that impulsivity is a stable characteristic of students with ADHD, they may not be aware that it is also a symptom seen in many students with ASD. Moreover, since impulsivity is associated with blurting out or acting out, it is often viewed as a behavior problem rather than a reflection of EF impairment. Hence, at this point we'd like to set forth an underlying theme that applies to all students with special needs: The first, most basic building block of appropriate IEP development and effective service delivery is knowledge of the specific disability and its symptoms, and an understanding of the way in which it affects the particular student who manifests it.

Based on this, we propose an underlying condition and annual goal (rendered in tongue-in-cheek fashion) to govern the performance of teachers and clinicians: Given basic knowledge of the specific disability (ASD, ADD/ADHD, NLD, S/LI, or ED) and the specific strengths, weaknesses, and needs of the student who manifests it, the teacher or clinician will make need-based educational decisions, on behalf of the student, across a variety of areas and domains that lead to appropriate service delivery.

> *The most basic building block of appropriate IEP development and effective service delivery is knowledge of the specific disability and its symptoms, and an understanding of the way in which it affects a particular student.*

Simply stated, without adequate knowledge of both the disability itself and the way in which it affects a particular student, it is impossible to determine the strategies, supports, or conditions that are helpful (or inimical) to the student. As noted previously, it is beyond the scope of this book to provide in-depth information on each of the conditions covered; however, we have listed several excellent resources for this purpose in Appendix B.

THE IMPORTANCE OF THE UNDERLYING CONDITION ON THE IEP

From the information provided thus far, it should be obvious that it is unacceptable to proceed without clarifying the underlying conditions for a student's performance, except in cases where they are so obvious that their inclusion would be ridiculous (as in the Mount Everest and tugboat examples). That said, it is better to err on the side of stating the obvious than to assume that the appropriate conditions for performance will be met when not specified. This will ensure that all objectives are being implemented in a consistent manner in the event of staff or programmatic change. Another reason why it is important to clearly articulate the underlying condition is that in some cases successful accomplishment of the objective is actually contingent upon it. Consider the following annual goal for a child with ADD:

> *Margaret will complete a multistep art project with a maximum of three reminders from staff.*

Anyone with knowledge of the organizational deficits that accompany ADD would know that, without the appropriate executive function supports, this goal would have a slim chance of being met. Clarifying the following appropriate underlying condition not only helps define the task for anyone working on the goal but also makes its successful accomplishment more likely:

> *Given a visual depiction (template) of the sequence of activities, Margaret will complete a multistep art project with a maximum of three reminders from staff.*

It should be obvious that, in this case, it is the underlying condition that actually makes the objective achievable, because the visual template provides the EF support that the student requires to be successful. Moreover, the underlying condition for performance serves to provide information to less knowledgeable staff regarding how to scaffold the student's performance.

VARIATIONS

Underlying conditions are usually specified in the first clause of the objective in order to emphasize what needs to be in place before performance is to be expected. Specific examples of some common underlying condition clauses will be given later in this chapter. It should be noted that most IEP forms also contain special sections where team members may specify accommodations and modifications. When specified, accommodations and modifications may be considered special types of underlying conditions because they delineate what the student needs in order to be successful. For example, if a Nerf® ball is to be used as an accommodation for softball or tennis in adaptive physical education, its use constitutes the condition under which performance in the particular sport is to be accomplished. It should be noted that listing accommodations elsewhere in the IEP does not take the place of including them as underlying conditions in IEP goals and objectives. For additional information on the role of accommodations and modifications, see Chapter Nine.

UNDERLYING CONDITIONS VERSUS METHODOLOGY

There may be a good deal of overlap between underlying conditions and methodology. Indeed, the line that distinguishes these two concepts is often blurry at best. For example, a particular methodology, such as the use of a Social Story™ (Gray, 2010) for a student with autism may also serve as a condition governing student performance. In this particular case, it really doesn't matter what you call it, because whether the Social Story™ serves as an underlying condition or as the methodology used to elicit certain behavior, all of the bases are covered. That said, there may be times when distinguishing between methodology and underlying conditions is advantageous. In that case, the following paragraph explains one way to distinguish between these interrelated concepts.

It may be useful to think of methodology as coming into play when one seeks to remediate a deficit. Underlying conditions, in contrast, may be thought of as compensatory strategies to circumvent the deficit area, promote acceptable task completion, or enable performance. For example, myopic or nearsighted individuals have difficulty seeing objects that are far away. Many myopic individuals compensate for their visual problems by wearing eyeglasses or contact lenses. These prosthetic devices are analogous to underlying conditions because they compensate for the nearsightedness and enable successful performance. It is important to note that the individual's visual acuity does not change, even though his or her visual performance does improve. In contrast, in recent years medical technology has introduced laser vision correction. It serves as a *method* for correcting or remediating the condition of nearsightedness. Similarly, an end-of-day checklist may serve as a prosthetic device for a student with ADHD with impaired executive skills. The brain function doesn't change, but the student's performance does as a result of the visual support. Likewise, teaching a student to use a chunking strategy is a method that can be used to improve rote memorization.

Although these examples provide a clear distinction between supports that compensate for weaknesses and enable performance (underlying conditions), and methods that remediate them (methodology), real-world distinctions between the two are not always clear-cut. So be it! The important point is this: in writing annual goals and short-term objectives it is important to cover the bases with respect to underlying conditions. If the underlying condition selected overlaps with methodology, think of it as accomplishing two important purposes for the "price" of one. For an in-depth discussion of methodology, see Chapter Four.

> *It may be useful to think of methodology as coming into play when one seeks to remediate a deficit; underlying conditions may be thought of as compensatory strategies.*

UNDERLYING CONDITIONS VERSUS PROMPTS

There is also a good deal of overlap between underlying conditions and prompts. Consider, for example, the following:

> *Given manual signs as cues for verbal expression, Meg will respond appropriately to social exchanges each time she is addressed.*

It should be obvious that the use of manual signs in this annual goal serves as both the condition for performance and the prompt that enables it. The following rule of thumb may be helpful in determining when a prompt is also an underlying condition. Because underlying conditions refer to those things that are done before a student is expected to perform a task, prompts that are given early on, as preconditions for performance, are likely doing double-duty—that is, they are serving as underlying conditions as well. But if the prompt is given after the student has been set up to succeed by a well-stated underlying condition, then it is likely serving as the cue for performance. Hence, the placement of the prompt in the IEP goal or objective (at the beginning or at the end) is often what determines its purpose—that is, as an underlying condition or a cue to prompt performance.

Finally, although fading back prompts is generally considered desirable, we caution against pulling the rug out from under students by precipitously and indiscriminately fading back prompts that may be essential underlying conditions for performance. Many students with ASD and ADD/ADHD have been ill-served when sorely needed organizational supports have been faded out, ostensibly to promote independence. Here's an example: Ross, a middle school student with high-functioning autism, was constantly being marked down in classes due to his difficulty completing and handing in homework assignments. This problem was solved when Ross was given a checklist to cue him to copy down the homework assignments after each class and take home the necessary materials to complete them. After two semesters, the school staff discontinued use of the checklist as a way to promote independence. Almost immediately, Ross began to miss his homework assignments and forget to take home the appropriate materials. It should be clear that Ross was demonstrating by his performance that he was unable to complete assignments without support for his organizational problems.

The preceding example illustrates two very important points. First, a student cannot be independent in a skill that he or she has not mastered (as Ross's performance in the absence of organizational supports clearly indicates). Second, because the EF problems seen in ADD/ADHD and ASD reflect deficits, as opposed to maturational issues, certain types of organizational supports, like checklists, are likely necessary in order for the student to be successful. Hence, we urge IEP teams to exercise both caution and discretion in this important issue, and to think long and hard about pulling away supports that may be necessary to successful performance. A far better approach would be to teach the student to independently use the supports that are necessary for his or her successful performance in order to have a life-long tool to shore up weaknesses in executive skills. A complete discussion of prompts and their relationship to student success is presented in Chapter Five.

> *Although fading back prompts is desirable, we caution against pulling the rug out from under students by precipitously and indiscriminately fading back prompts that may be essential underlying conditions for performance.*

EXAMPLES OF UNDERLYING CONDITIONS

The underlying conditions that one selects should be based on well-established compensatory strategies or other contingencies deemed crucial to student success. Following is a list of commonly used underlying conditions. This is not a complete list of all the possible underlying conditions that may be effective for students but instead is designed to "prompt" the reader to think about the types of conditions that may be necessary for successful performance. We encourage creativity and specificity when determining underlying conditions on the theory, as we have explained, that well-stated underlying conditions help to set up a student for successful performance. That said, preceded by the word *given,* one or more of the following may serve as underlying conditions in IEP goals and objectives:

- Visual supports

- A visual schedule

- A timer that depicts the passage of time visually

- Direct instruction/teaching

- Desirable options

- A social script

- A list of written rules

- A model

- A template

- A social cue card

- Manual signs

WRAPPING UP THE MAIN POINTS

- When IEP teams write annual goals and short-term objectives, it is essential that they consider and include those factors that enable successful student performance.

- Knowing the symptoms and characteristics associated with students' disabilities, as well as how they affect individual students, is key to providing informed and appropriate educational support.

- It may be advantageous to distinguish between underlying conditions and methodology. Supports that compensate for weaknesses and enable performance are underlying conditions; techniques and strategies that remediate them are considered methodology.

- Underlying conditions should be stated within each goal and objective to set up the student for successful performance and ensure consistency across staff.

CHAPTER

4

METHODOLOGY: NO LONGER A SACRED COW

"Though this be madness yet there is method in it."

—*William Shakespeare,* Hamlet

Despite the new language in IDEA 2004 that rejects the viewpoint that methodology is the exclusive domain of school districts, it is a position to which school districts adhere with a tenacity rivaling pit bulls. As a result, some refuse even to discuss methodology at the IEP meeting. Other, more accommodating districts will listen to parents' concerns as a courtesy but ultimately reserve their perceived right to determine instructional methods on their own. Yet, such a unilateral position on methodology is not only unwise but also incorrect. While there may be "wiggle room" on the question of whether to include information on instructional methodology in the IEP document, the new language in IDEA 2004 strongly favors doing so. In fact, Wayne Steedman (Fall/Winter, 2005), a special education attorney with Wrightslaw—arguably the most respected group of education-law attorneys in the nation—states that the law's "frequent reference to research-based instruction and interventions makes it clear that this is an area Congress considered vitally important" (p. 23). Moreover, Steedman (Fall/Winter, 2005) goes on to say that "the IEP must include 'a statement of special education and related services and supplementary aids and services, based on peer reviewed research to the extent practicable to be provided to the child' § 1414(d)(1)(A)(i)(IV)" (p. 23).

By requiring instructional methodology to be research-based, IDEA 2004 has left open the door for greater scrutiny of the extent to which specific methods fit this requirement. In addition, an off-limits approach to either discussing methodology or including it in the IEP document would seem not only to violate the spirit of IDEA 2004, which is to treat parents as equal partners in the IEP process, but also to undermine a collegial relationship between educators and parents. Finally, whereas methodology for some academic subjects is circumscribed by the particular reading or math program adopted by the school district, this is not the case for the "subjects" that fall into the categories of executive function, theory of mind, and others addressed in Part Two of the current volume. In fact, because skills that fall into these categories are not typically addressed in schools, collaboration on methodology to address specific areas of deficit seems not only appropriate but also wise.

> *An off-limits approach to either discussing methodology or including it in the IEP document would seem not only to violate the spirit of IDEA 2004, which is to treat parents as equal partners in the IEP process, but also to undermine a collegial relationship between educators and parents.*

INFLUENCES FROM THE PAST

The reason why some school districts consider methodology to be in their sole discretion is rooted in educational tradition: because schools were traditionally charged with the mission of educating students, they were also deemed to be the "keepers of the flame" when it came to methodology. This stance was consistent with the sentiments of parents of an earlier age, when they willingly left the business of education to the educators alone. But times have changed. Accordingly, the very idea of methodology being the sacred cow of the school district—or of any one party, for that matter—is antithetical to the collaborative spirit of IDEA 2004.

Because of the nature of the disabilities discussed in this book—especially ASD—specific instructional methods are often needed if the student is to receive an appropriate education. Why? Because the students with the conditions covered in this book often manifest difficulty in arcane areas of functioning that are not typically addressed in schools. For example, nondisabled students absorb theory of mind knowledge as if by osmosis, without need for the school to directly address it. The same is true for social information, several areas of critical thinking, and other aspects of cognitive and social-cognitive functioning. This is why we feel that discussion of, and collaboration on, decisions about instructional methodology that is usually outside of the standard curriculum is in

The reason why some school districts consider methodology to be their sole discretion is rooted in the educational tradition of being "the keepers of the flame."

the best educational interests of the student. Steedman (Fall/Winter, 2005) supports this position with the following statement: "Including methodology in the IEP is an advantage to parents and teachers alike. . . . It's a win-win situation for all—especially the child" (p. 23).

IN SEARCH OF CLARITY

Methodological issues are not always clear-cut. At the most basic level is the question of what exactly constitutes methodology. We've often found that methodology is in the "eye of the beholder" and sometimes mistaken for something else. One person's methodology may be another person's underlying condition, and with good reason, for as noted in Chapter Three, there is a good deal of overlap between the two concepts (a point that will be further elaborated elsewhere in this book).

To ensure that everyone is on the same page when it comes to this important but nebulous concept, a few definitions are in order. *The New Lexicon Webster's Dictionary of the English Language* (Cayne, 1989) defines *method* as "a way of doing something or a procedure for doing something" (p. 628). Similarly, it defines the closely related term *technique* as "the entire body of procedures and methods" (p. 1015). The more general term *methodology* is defined as "a system of methods" (p. 628). For our purposes here we use the terms *methods, techniques*, and *procedures* interchangeably as the discrete components that constitute what is known more generally as *methodology*.

A MEANS-ENDS PROPOSITION

Now that the terms have been defined, let's delve into the issue of why careful consideration of methodology is central to the concept of appropriate education, and why it is particularly crucial in the case of students with the conditions we address here. As for appropriate education, one can look to the landmark Supreme

Court case known as *Board of Education v. Rowley* (1982). Specifically, the *educational benefit* standard set forth in that case not only has important implications for methodology but also ties it to the concept of an appropriate education. According to that Supreme Court decision, "Implicit in the congressional purpose of providing access to a 'free appropriate public education' is the requirement that the education to which access is provided be sufficient to confer some *educational benefit* [italics added] upon the handicapped child" (as cited in Wright and Wright, 1999, p. 311). It should be obvious that inappropriate methods and techniques would be inimical to the standard of educational benefit. Furthermore, it is impossible to envision how inappropriate means (methods) could result in appropriate ends (educational benefit).

Although we feel that collaborating on methodology is important for all of the students discussed in this book, it is especially important for students with ASD, given the enigmatic and unpredictable nature of autism spectrum conditions. Consequently, teaching methods and procedures that are appropriate for students with other disabilities—and even for some with ASD—are often distinctly inappropriate for particular students with ASD (Peeters and Gillberg, 1999). For example, traditional, hands-on preschool activities such as finger painting and working with glue would be off-putting, and hence unsuitable, for a child with ASD who has significant tactile defensiveness. Similarly, it is not uncommon to be blinded by the strengths in procedural knowledge and unmindful of the weaknesses in declarative knowledge in high-functioning students with ASD, and to unknowingly employ teaching methods that actually require them to perform at levels precluded by their disability. For example, a more able, hyperlexic, preschool child with ASD may decode words at a third- or fourth-grade level. Blinded by the child's strengths in decoding, and unmindful that hyperlexia, by definition, carries with it problems in reading comprehension, a teacher might assume normal or advanced ability in understanding where it does not exist. Under this misapprehension, educators could require the child to perform at a level beyond his or her capacity. Likewise, a lack of understanding of ASD in general, or of some of the

> *"Implicit in the congressional purpose of providing access to a 'free appropriate public education' is the requirement that the education to which access is provided be sufficient to confer some* educational benefit *upon the handicapped child."*

more subtle symptoms in particular, could cause well-meaning but unaware school personnel to either use methods that are inimical to a student's best interests or fail to employ those that have been found to be successful with this population. <u>It could also cause school staff to misjudge the student's efforts, and to label him or her as unmotivated, or worse, noncompliant.</u>

It should be noted that although the needs of students with ASD are often more difficult to decipher than those of students with other disabilities, this does not insulate students with ADD/ADHD, NLD, S/LI, or ED from similar misunderstandings. The examples that follow draw attention to the deleterious effect that a lack of knowledge about the student's disability may have on methodology selection.

EXAMPLES FROM THE TRENCHES

The following vignettes illustrate the important link between methodology and outcomes.

VIGNETTE 1

Maureen is a sixth-grade student with high-functioning ASD. Although she is able to answer questions from her reading book that are concrete and factual, she has great difficulty in answering questions that require her to infer from the information given, that which is not immediately available in the text. Determining that the area of inference-making constitutes a priority educational need, Maureen's IEP team developed the following annual goal:

> *Given 10 grade-level reading passages, Maureen will answer inference-based questions with 90% accuracy.*

Despite the clearly stated underlying condition, straightforward student outcome, and clear performance criterion, Maureen made virtually no progress on this objective in an entire year. She also experienced tremendous frustration with respect to it. An examination of the methods that the teacher was using with Maureen is instructive here. Instead of providing her with lower-level, more "concrete" inferences as a starting place (for example, "Why did John take the book out of the library?") and then having her select the correct answer in a multiple-choice format, her teacher jumped straight to the top of the inference hierarchy by selecting those having to do with mental states ("How did Mary *feel* when her mother told her that she couldn't buy a new dress?"). She then required Maureen to answer the question as it was presented orally, without benefit of a less challenging multiple-choice format.

This example illustrates how student performance can be compromised by inappropriate methodology—in this case inappropriate vis-à-vis the complexity of the material. It also illustrates how a lack of knowledge about ASD can jeopardize educational outcomes. Here, the lack of knowledge was evident on two fronts. First, the underlying condition assumed that inference-making is related to grade level, and second, the choice of the particular inferential material (determining mental states) indicated a lack of understanding of the critical role of theory of mind deficits in ASD. It should be apparent from this vignette that a lack of knowledge of ASD can set up a kind of domino-like effect, in which the selection of inappropriate methods leads to unsuccessful outcomes.

VIGNETTE 2

Lucy is a preschool child with moderate to severe autism who cannot tolerate morning circle for more than three to five minutes at a time without engaging in highly disruptive behavior.

The IEP team determined that a priority educational need for Lucy was to increase her ability to tolerate morning circle without disrupting the teacher or her classmates. Hence, it generated the following annual goal:

Lucy will be able to stay in morning circle for 10 minutes without disrupting her classmates or teacher.

The lack of an underlying condition should serve as a red flag, because there are a number of ways to accomplish something, not all of which may be appropriate. In this case, Lucy did accomplish the objective but her "achievement" came at a cost. In order to enable Lucy to remain in the circle activity for the length of time specified, her paraprofessional support assistant—with the blessing of the teacher—allowed Lucy to tune out the activity and engage in self-stimulatory behavior in the form of saliva play. The adage "At what price glory" comes to mind!

> ## VIGNETTE 3
>
> Mark is a fourth-grade student with ADHD whose teachers describe him as irresponsible. As evidence, they cite his messy desk, his proclivity for losing things, his "blurting things out" even after several reminders to raise his hand, and his failure to complete and turn in his homework.
>
> Based on this description, the IEP team generated the following annual goal:
>
> *Mark will keep track of his belongings, keep his desk neat, and turn in his homework assignments on time.*

The description of Mark reveals a great deal about the IEP team's knowledge base (or lack thereof). Specifically, there is no acknowledgment that any of the behaviors they described are classic symptoms of EF difficulty in individuals with ADHD. Use of the term *irresponsible* to describe Mark underscores this point. By putting the entire onus for his organizational issues on Mark, the school relinquishes its responsibility for providing the EF props (such as checklists, homework support strategies, and the like) needed to accomplish its objective. Clearly, an appropriate underlying condition for this annual goal would be *given organizational supports.*

These examples illustrate the educational havoc wreaked by inappropriate methodology (and a whole lot more), not only in terms of student performance and progress but also in terms of student well-being. As for the latter, the unfortunate result of holding students to specific standards without providing the supports needed to reach them is increased stress and anxiety. It should also be apparent that the thread of commonality running through these three examples, and through those given previously, is that when there is a lack of knowledge or understanding of the students' disability, there is concomitant difficulty in selecting appropriate methods and procedures to teach them. The importance of this point cannot be overstated, particularly because many of the deficit areas in ASD, ADD/ADHD, NLD, S/LI, and ED require specialized knowledge and understanding—say, for example, in theory of mind and executive functioning—beyond that which many college special education programs typically provide. In addition, these deficit areas require specific and direct attention over and above that which is needed by typically developing students. Considering today's emphasis on inclusive education, both of these factors are particularly problematic for regular education teachers. Specifically, many do not understand, and hence are ill-equipped to deal with some of the cognitive and social-cognitive challenges manifested by students with these types of deficits. Absent such knowledge, they are likely to look upon impairment in theory of mind or executive functioning as a behavioral issue. One way that school districts have addressed this problem is by assigning special educators to team-teach classes alongside regular educators. Depending on the expertise of the special educator and the dynamics of the team members' relationship, this can either be highly successful or laborious and cumbersome.

To clarify our position on methodology, we recommend the following:

- All members of the IEP team should have sufficient knowledge of the student's disability to be able to determine his or her educational needs.

- All team members should be sufficiently familiar with relevant research findings to be able to select research-based methodology appropriate to the student's needs.

- The idea that methodology is the exclusive domain of any one party—school or parent—should be laid to rest.

- There should be a frank and open discussion about methodology during the IEP meeting, as a backdrop for joint input and decision making.

- Where feasible, there should be a description of the methodology to be used with the student in the IEP document. (This can be included in the goals and objectives themselves or specified elsewhere. This description need not be detailed or complex, and it should be of sufficient flexibility so as not to tie the hands of the teaching and clinical staff.)

- Members of the IEP team should acknowledge—by the time and attention they devote to methodological considerations—that effective service delivery can only occur in the presence of appropriate methods and procedures.

Members of the IEP team should acknowledge that effective service delivery can only occur in the presence of appropriate methods and procedures.

MORE EXAMPLES OF UNDERLYING CONDITIONS

A few more examples of the similarities and differences between underlying conditions and methodology, in addition to those discussed in Chapter Three, may be helpful. Consider, for example, the following:

> *Given a joint activity snack routine, Michael will request desired items from a group of three food choices 90% of the time.*

It should be obvious that the phrase *given a joint activity snack routine* is both a condition for performance (that is, the appearance of the skill— *requesting* — requires this context) and a social-pragmatic technique for teaching students to request. In contrast, consider this example:

> *Given a board game, Amy will take turns with one partner 90% of the time without verbal reminders.*

Is the phrase beginning with the word *given* a condition or a statement of methodology? We would characterize it as a condition for performance rather than as a method for teaching the behavior (that Amy will take turns in a board game activity rather than in some other context.). Why? Although the goal specifies the context in which turn-taking will, one hopes, occur, it is silent on the issue of how the turn-taking behavior will be taught. The operative word here is *how* —that is, if the phrase beginning with the word *given* specifies information relating to how the skill will be taught, as opposed to simply articulating the conditions under which it will be performed, then it addresses methodology. The following example includes both the condition for performance and the method for teaching the turn-taking behavior:

> *Given a board game and the use of a turn marker, Amy will demonstrate the ability to take turns by passing the marker to her partner at the appropriate times with 90% accuracy.*

Clearly, the board game serves as the underlying condition (the context) for performance, whereas the use of a turn marker (for example, a small circle with the words *my turn* written on it) serves as the method for concretizing and teaching the turn-taking behavior. It should also be apparent that the more specificity there is in the goal or objective, the greater the guidance to the educator or clinician carrying it out, and the more comprehensible it is for everyone involved.

WRAPPING UP THE MAIN POINTS

- Because of the nature of the disabilities covered in this book, highly specific instructional methods are often needed for students to receive an appropriate education.

- Methodological considerations have enormous significance for these students, as well as momentous implications for the delivery of appropriate educational services.

- By requiring methods to be based on research evidence, IDEA 2004 holds methodology to a higher standard than in previous versions of the law.

- Although educators have some leeway with respect to methodology, they are not given license to be the sole determiners of the methods and techniques to be used to address skill development. That responsibility rests with the IEP team, of which parents are an integral part.

- Although the decision to include instructional methodology in the IEP document is left to the discretion of the IEP team, we believe that doing so is by far in the best educational interests of the student.

CHAPTER

SCAFFOLDING STUDENT SUCCESS

"If you can't describe what you are doing as a process, you don't know what you are doing."

—*W. Edwards Deming*

IDEA 2004 clearly states that IEP annual goals must be measurable. And as discussed previously, we know that a student's present level of academic achievement and functional performance (PLP) is the standard against which progress is to be judged. In this chapter we discuss the importance of using appropriate criteria for measurement as well as how prompt levels relate to academic and functional performance.

DETERMINING CRITERIA

The term *criteria* has a decidedly quantitative ring to it, conjuring up images of numbers and other mathematical symbols. Such criteria as percentages (80 percent), or number of trials (four out of five times), are standard fare in most IEPs. Other criteria, though important, are specified less frequently. These include the number of times a behavior should be performed (five times per day) or a specific time frame for performance (for a minimum of ten minutes). All of these measurements provide different ways of assessing a student's progress toward mastery of the annual goal.

Although many goals readily lend themselves to these standard units of measurement, many others do not. For example, the speech of some more able individuals with ASD may be characterized by inappropriate prosody (for example, monotone or singsong intonation). Difficulty in this area is not easy to assess, or characterize, because prosody is really the end product of many important sub-skills that interact with each other, including rhythm, rate, volume, tone of voice, stress patterns, and so on. Furthermore, determining appropriate prosody requires a subjective judgment that is not consistent with straightforward quantitative measures such as percentages. Unfortunately, measurement "purists" have often steered clear of writing objectives for behaviors that are not quantifiable. This is akin to throwing out the baby with the bathwater, particularly with respect to the skill areas that need to be addressed among students with the conditions covered in this book, because many of them cannot be quantified.

Another problem with criteria is that in attempting to carry out the measurability requirements of IDEA 2004, the IEP team sometimes (often?) selects measures that are inappropriate or even nonsensical. Consider, for example, the following:

> *Given appropriate visual cues, Blake will use appropriate prosody with 80% accuracy.*

Despite the quantitative ring that the 80 percent lends to the objective, *accuracy* (whatever that means in this particular case) will undoubtedly be "in the ear of the beholder," and sketchy at that. Moreover, one needs to ask, "Eighty percent of what?"

How then does the IEP team meet its obligation under IDEA 2004 to measure student performance when the skill to be measured doesn't lend itself to quantification? One way is to design a system other than quantification for determining progress toward the annual goal for these kinds of behaviors. In the prosody example, one might design a rating scale that can be used to judge the quality of the student's speech according to specified parameters, such as volume, rate, stress patterns, and so on. Qualitative means of evaluation will be discussed later in this chapter and also in Chapter Eight.

The measurement of multidimensional skills presents a particularly thorny problem, and also makes the case for using short-term objectives to monitor progress toward the annual goal. Consider the following annual goal (offered with tongue in cheek) to illustrate not only the outrageous outcome that misapplied criteria can cause but also to delineate the use of a task analysis for multidimensional skills:

> *Carrie will safely cross the street four out of five (4/5) times.*

The goal, as stated, does not measure functional performance in a meaningful way. Clearly, Carrie could meet the goal yet still meet with disaster on the fifth trial. In addition, the term *safely* is vague. After all, Carrie may be able to cross an empty street without being hurt, even if she doesn't stop to look for oncoming cars. Moreover, this goal does not specify the degree of assistance that she will need to accomplish the task. Although independence is always an important goal, it is advisable to scaffold Carrie's performance by providing the supervision or assistance that she will need in the early stages of skill development. A simple task analysis—that is, breakdown of the behavior into its components—solves the measurement problem. (The underlying conditions for performance also help!) For example:

> *Given direct teaching and modeling, a set of rules for crossing the street safely, and adult supervision, Carrie will*
>
> 1. *Stop at the curb;*
> 2. *Look both ways;*
> 3. *Wait until there are no oncoming cars;*
> 4. *Cross the street in a timely fashion*
>
> *in 4/5 opportunities, with gradually decreasing prompts, moving from physical assistance to independence.*

Note that short-term objectives could be written for performing the task first in various role-play situations.

The four behaviors addressed in this objective constitute both the specific behaviors that will be directly taught and the outcomes by which the student's progress toward the annual goal will be measured over time. This objective also contains other important features. The phrase *gradually decreasing prompts, moving from physical assistance to independence* ensures that progress will also be judged by the degree to which the student moves toward independent performance. In addition, the underlying conditions provide guidance for caregivers by clearly delineating the types of supports that Carrie will need in order to accomplish the goal of crossing the street safely. Given the specificity of the behaviors being measured and the clearly defined supports for performance, the four out of five opportunities criterion level no longer comes across as unrealistic or non-sensical, particularly when short-term objectives first address skill acquisition in role-play situations.

This example also illustrates two interrelated and important points:

1. In order for criteria to be useful, they must be able to measure gains in student performance in a meaningful way.

2. Sometimes it is necessary to break down multidimensional behavior (that is, perform a task analysis) in order to measure functional performance in a meaningful way.

Finally, it should be apparent from the foregoing discussion that three elements impact the specification of criteria in an IEP goal or objective:

1. The behaviors to be measured must be clearly delineated.

2. The criteria for measuring those behaviors must be appropriate and clearly specified.

3. The level of prompting or support for skill development must be addressed to ensure progress toward independence.

Each of these elements will be considered separately in the next sections.

Although many goals readily lend themselves to standard units of measurement, many others do not.

DELINEATING BEHAVIORS

When annual goals are too global it is not only difficult to select ways to address them but also likely that they will be addressed differently by different people. Consider the case of four-year-old Sarah. Her PLP states that she is able to put circles, triangles, and squares on a form board independently but has difficulty with other cutouts. The IEP team determines that learning to do puzzles is both age-appropriate and an activity that will enable Sarah to make progress in the preschool curriculum alongside her peers. The team generates the following annual goal:

Given any ten-piece puzzle, Sarah will independently put it together 9/10 times.

Without a written plan in the form of short-term objectives that delineate the specific behavioral steps toward completion of the goal, those working with Sarah may approach the task at a level that is above her ability to succeed. For example, her paraprofessional support assistant may put a blank ten-piece puzzle frame in front of her and use hand-over-hand prompting to help her to put the pieces in place. Her teacher may present her with a partially completed puzzle and use hand-over-hand prompting to help her put just the last three pieces in place. Unfortunately, given Sarah's lack of success with shapes other than circles, squares, and triangles (as noted in her PLP), neither the teacher's nor the paraprofessional's approach to the task is likely to be successful, because both begin at a place that is well above Sarah's functioning level. This situation (and the frustration that accompanies it) can be avoided by delineating the behaviors that will move Sarah toward the accomplishment of the annual goal in a series of short-term objectives. Consider the following:

> Given a shape sorter with a variety of shapes, Sarah will put the shapes in the correct places with gradually decreasing prompts from physical assistance to gestures 9/10 times.

> Given a form board, Sarah will put cutouts of animals in the appropriate places with gradually decreasing prompts from gestures to expectant waiting 9/10 trials.

> Given a five-piece puzzle, Sarah will complete the puzzle with minimal gestural cues to expectant waiting 9/10 trials.

> Given a ten-piece puzzle, Sarah will complete the puzzle independently 9/10 trials.

> Given a variety of ten-piece puzzles, Sarah will complete the puzzles independently 9/10 trials.

With the final short-term objective, Sarah meets the annual goal that was listed.

There are three advantages to using short-term objectives to delineate the behaviors that will help move the student toward achievement of the goal: First, doing so will ensure that each individual working on the goal will begin where the learner is (not where he or she isn't!) in ability level. Second, it will ensure consistency among staff in their approach to teaching the skill. Third, it will serve as a road map for reaching the destination (achievement of the annual goal).

The following are general reminders for IEP team members:

1. When a behavior has several components, list each of the components that will be measured separately. Some examples of multicomponent behaviors are

   - Using a visual schedule
   - Completing an art project

- Writing a story

- Completing activities of daily living (ADLs: washing clothes or dishes, vacuuming, making a bed, and so on)

- Self-care skills (toileting, brushing teeth, dressing, and so on)

- Buying an item at a store

- Going to a restaurant

- Carrying on a conversation

- Solving a problem

2. When several levels of performance are possible within a skill, clarify the intent of the goal or objective by specifying the level at which the student is expected to perform, as noted parenthetically in the following examples:

- Following directions (one-step versus two-step versus three-step)

- Understanding concepts (core versus concrete versus abstract)

- Conversing (for how many conversational turns?)

Careful consideration of the foregoing will go a long way toward ensuring that the behaviors leading to successful student performance are clearly delineated. Furthermore, going through this process also helps ensure that all staff working on the particular goal will be on the same wavelength!

MEASUREMENT CRITERIA: A NUMBERS GAME

Although the topic of measurement is discussed at length in Chapter Eight, a few points are in order here. Once the desired student behavior is clearly specified, the next step is to determine the appropriate criterion for measurement. IEP teams have many options. For example, if the behavior is trial-based (the student is expected to perform the behavior a specific number of times), the following means may be used to define criteria:

- Percentage (for example, 80 percent of trials)

- Fraction (four out of five [4/5] times)

- Specific number of times (five times per day)

For other behaviors, explicit time periods may be more appropriate. Consider the following time-based measurements:

- Specific amount of time (for a minimum of ten minutes, within five seconds, and so on)

- Relative time frames (five minutes per hour, four times per school day, and so on)

In still other instances, quantitative measurement may need to give way to qualitative indicators of progress. For example, Likert or other rating scales provide qualitative information on performance. These can be used to judge speech measures that do not lend themselves to quantification, such as *prosody* and *intelligibility*.

Once the desired student behavior is clearly specified, the next step is to determine the appropriate criterion for measurement.

SPECIFYING PROMPT LEVELS

Most parents and professionals would agree that successful student performance is not only based on the appearance of a particular skill but also on the degree to which the skill can be [performed independently] Indeed, mastery of a skill demands independent performance.

Typically developing children move toward independence quite easily. For example, one of the reasons the "two's" have come to be characterized as "terrible" is that the child's inexorable move toward independence becomes eminently obvious at that stage of development. To wit, the well-known two-year-old child's definitive declaration, "Do by myself!"

Some children with special needs, however, find the journey from supported skill acquisition to independent functioning a long and arduous one. This is especially true for students on the autism spectrum, particularly those who are at the less able end of the autism continuum. These individuals often demonstrate an inordinate reliance on specific cues and prompts for successful performance. Therefore, students with ASD are commonly referred to as *prompt-dependent*. Over the years, this term has become nearly synonymous with the spectrum of autism (Carr and Kologinsky, 1983; Rincover and Koegel, 1975; Woods, 1987); that is, many individuals on the autism spectrum possess skills they cannot perform in the absence of cues or prompts, even though these may be very subtle.

When IEP goals or objectives do not specify prompt levels, adults may use varying levels of cueing (some of which may be highly intrusive) to elicit target behaviors. This can and often does set the stage for prompt dependency, or worse yet, *learned helplessness*. The latter may be considered the final stage of prompt dependency in which the student does virtually nothing without prompting. It is important to note that although students with ASD are notoriously prone to prompt dependence and learned helplessness, both of these behaviors may be manifested by students with other conditions if adults do not exercise careful attention to fading back prompts and promoting independent performance. Considering the importance of this endeavor to the mastery of skills, it is critical that IEP teams not only specify prompt levels for annual goals and short-term objectives but also develop a plan for systematically fading them back to facilitate independence and self-efficacy in the student.

There are several places on the IEP form where prompt levels may be listed. They are most advantageously listed in the body of the goal and objective, as indicated throughout this book. Such placement helps keep them front-and-center. On many IEP forms, however, there is a separate box in which to list criteria and prompt levels. The important thing to remember is that, regardless of where they are listed in the IEP document, these essential elements of the IEP (criteria and prompt levels) must never be left to chance.

A PROMPT HIERARCHY

To ensure that prompts are faded back effectively, a specific prompt hierarchy should be specified for each annual goal and objective. The following is an annotated list of common prompt levels, arranged in descending order from independence to dependence. (It should be noted that even though we consider gestural cues, manual signs, and visual cues to represent the same prompt level, we separate them here as a convenience to the reader.)

- *Independent/initiated:* No prompts are given to the student, because he or she is expected to perform the task independently.

- *Expectant waiting/expectant time delay:* The adult pauses with a look of anticipation and arms raised expectantly to give the student additional time and impetus to respond.

- *Gestural cues:* The adult uses body movements such as

  - Social referencing by shifting one's gaze or moving one's head from student to object or activity

- Pointing

- Shrugging one's shoulders

- Shaking one's head, *No*

- Nodding one's head, *Yes*

- *Manual signs:* Such as those used in American Sign Language.

- *Visual cues:* The student is shown a representational object or picture to cue him or her to perform a specific behavior.

- *Verbal cues:* The adult uses his or her voice to cue the student. Examples include

  - Repetition of directions

  - Verbal instruction (*direct:* "Check your schedule"; *indirect:* "What do you need to do?")

  - Verbal model of language

  - Provision of phonemic/sound cues

  - Cloze sentences (use of automatic fill-in responses such as, *There is someone at the . . .*)

  - Questions

- *Combinations of cues:* At times, a student may need a variety of different cues (tactile, verbal, gestural, and so on) in order to perform a behavior. These may be referred to as

  - Multisensory cues

  - Tactile and visual cues

  - Visual and verbal cues

- *Physical cues/assistance:* The adult touches the student or physically guides him or her through a desired behavior. (Hand-over-hand assistance is one of the most intrusive types of physical prompts.)

Table 5.1 assigns levels to the prompt categories in order to provide the reader with a ready-to-use format for writing annual goals and short-term objectives. In some cases, there may be overlap between categories. In others, further individualization in the form of interim steps or additional input may be

TABLE 5.1   A PROMPT HIERARCHY

Level 0	Independent performance/initiation
Level 1	Expectant waiting/expectant time delay
Level 2	Gestures, manual signs, or visual cues
Level 3	Verbal cues
Level 4	Combination of cues (verbal and manual signs)
Level 5	Physical cues/assistance

Note: Level 0 indicates that no prompts are to be used, because independent performance/initiation is required.

needed. We leave decisions about such individualization to the discretion of the IEP team.

To determine the necessary level of prompting, select the lowest-level prompt capable of eliciting the desired behavior and move toward greater independence over time, keeping in mind that the selection of prompt levels is always governed by student performance.

The following is an example of how the information in Table 5.1 may be applied. If the PLP for a student states that the child grabs food items that she wants in the absence of appropriately requesting them, the annual goal might be for her to initiate requests for food items by independently handing a picture card to the teacher. The short-term objectives would target various aspects of skill acquisition, and in this case they would involve gradually decreasing prompts on the way to independent performance. To illustrate how the level of prompting would decrease, we offer a series of objectives in service to the annual goal of *requesting*. The format in which we choose to teach this skill is that of the joint activity snack routine. The first objective would contain the most intrusive prompt needed, with subsequent objectives indicating less intrusive prompt levels:

> *To determine the necessary level of prompting, select the lowest-level prompt capable of eliciting the desired behavior and move toward greater independence over time.*

Objective 1: Level 5 prompt (physical assistance): Teacher says or signs, "What do you want?" and paraprofessional physically assists student to give picture of desired snack item to teacher, nine out of ten times.

Objective 2: Level 5 less intrusive physical assistance prompt: Teacher says or signs, "What do you want?" and paraprofessional taps child's arm to cue student to give the picture of the item to the teacher, nine out of ten times.

Objective 3: Level 4 prompt (combination of cues): Teacher holds hand out as he or she says, "What do you want?" and student hands picture of requested snack item nine out of ten times.

Objective 4: Level 3 prompt with expectant time delay: Teacher says, "What do you want?" while waiting expectantly.

Objective 5: Level 2 prompt: Teacher gestures toward the snack tray and waits expectantly.

Objective 6: Level 1 (initiation): Teacher presents snack tray and waits for the child to request (that is, hand the picture to the teacher independently to request a desired food item).

It should be obvious that Objective 6 would, with proper wording, constitute the annual goal.

The foregoing illustrates and specifically delineates the systematic progression from intrusive prompting to independent performance. For those readers who stubbornly refuse to include short-term objectives for students taking standard assessments—notwithstanding our strong recommendation to do so—the following phrase may be inserted at the end of the annual goal: *with gradually decreasing prompts beginning with such and such (for example, verbal prompts) and extending to such and such (independence).* Criteria and prompt levels like the following illustrate how the fading back of prompts may be characterized in an annual goal:

- Eight out of ten opportunities per week, with gradually decreasing prompts from verbal to gestural cues to expectant waiting and independent performance

- A rating scale performance of at least 4, given a progression over time from manual signs to expectant time delay to spontaneous production of appropriate response

It should be apparent that prompts provide useful information on both student performance expectations and teaching strategies. Furthermore, they also help ensure that adults overseeing the student's educational programming do not become complacent in maintaining intrusive prompt levels beyond the point that they are necessary. Finally, it is important to keep in mind that successful performance is determined not only by the appearance of a particular skill but also by the extent to which that skill is performed independently.

WRAPPING UP THE MAIN POINTS

- IDEA 2004 clearly states that IEP annual goals must be measurable. It is therefore critical to develop functional and meaningful criteria by which to measure annual goals and short-term objectives.

- IEP teams must delineate the specific behaviors needed to move the student toward achievement of the annual goal and also specify the criteria that will be used to measure progress.

- Specifying prompt levels—beginning with the least intrusive prompt capable of cueing performance and developing a plan for systematically fading prompts back to achieve skill mastery—is of utmost importance.

CHAPTER

THE CASE FOR GENERALIZATION

"Begin with the end in mind."

—*Stephen R. Covey,* The 7 Habits of Highly Effective People

In his acclaimed book *The 7 Habits of Highly Effective People*, Stephen Covey (1989) listed as one of the now-famous seven habits the importance of beginning "with the end in mind" (p. 95). We attach the same degree of importance to this practice in the delivery of appropriate educational services. In our opinion, beginning with the end in mind means that we must not only pay careful attention to the generalization of skills but that we must do so at the *beginning* of the teaching process, not just at the end. The importance of generalization cannot be overstated, because skills that can only be performed in specific settings, or with only one person, or in one type of activity, are neither functional nor truly mastered.

The term *generalization* refers to the transference of the acquired skill or skills to other settings, activities, and people. Students with ASD have well-known problems with generalization. Hence, specific attention to the generalization of skills is critical for this population. That said, attention to generalization is also important for students with ADD/ADHD, NLD, S/LI, and ED.

The paucity of attention given to generalization belies its importance. For example, how functional would it be for a student to be able to request food items only from his teacher or only while seated at the horseshoe-shaped table in the classroom during snack time? In the autism community, these examples are by no means far-fetched, because students with ASD have a situation-specific, rigid learning style that does not easily accommodate the generaliza-

The term generalization *refers to the transference of the acquired skill or skills to other settings, activities, and people.*

tion of skills across people, settings, and activities. Similarly, how functional would it be for a student with ADHD or social-emotional difficulty to apply problem-solving strategies only in school, or for those with NLD or language-learning difficulties to be able to appreciate paralinguistic cues only in the therapy room? Clearly, although specific attention to generalization is imperative for students with ASD, programming for generalization should occur for all students with special needs in order to ensure skill mastery and functional performance across people, activities, and settings.

GENERALIZATION DIFFERENCES BETWEEN ASD AND OTHER CONDITIONS

A tremendous amount of research documents the profound generalization needs of students with ASD (Gaylord-Ross, Haring, Breen, and Pitts-Conway, 1984; Gena, Krantz, McClannahan, and Poulson, 1996; Koegel, Koegel, and O'Neill, 1989; Ihrig and Wolchik, 1988; Taylor and Harris, 1995). In fact, problems in generalization are considered endemic in this population. This is not to say that generalization of skills should be assumed for students with other disabilities, for clearly that is not the case. However, the problems with generalization seen in students on the autism spectrum are not only different from but also go well beyond the scope of those of students with other disabilities. Specifically, where students with ADD/ADHD, NLD, S/LI, and ED may have problems generalizing certain skills, their transference problems appear to be rooted in more "superficial" circumstances—for example, in external conditions such as inattention, forgetfulness, distractibility, or working-memory problems. In contrast, students with ASD have deep-seated systemic problems with generalization that appear to be "wired in" to the disability. There are deficits inherent in the disorder itself that can actually preclude such individuals from independently connecting up disparate pieces of information in order to form a generalized concept. For example, stimulus overselectivity is a well-recognized feature of autism in which the student overfocuses on one small feature or component of an object or event. The item of focus is usually irrelevant and often related to the student's idiosyncratic interests. Such a narrow focus interferes with the establishment of meaning, because the relevant cues that enable understanding are ignored. Stimulus overselectivity can interfere with the generalization of skills to an unfamiliar environment if the student, overfocusing on an irrelevant detail, ignores the relevant cues that are intended to prompt the learned behavior in the new setting. There are many other reasons for the generalization problems that occur in ASD, including difficulty making appropriate connections and problems recognizing the need for the new behavior in a different environment or activity.

Generalization difficulty is not confined only to traditional academic subjects but also extends to such areas of functioning as executive function, communication and language, social skills, critical thinking, and other developmental domains, many of which loom large for individuals with the conditions covered in this book. Olley and Stevenson (1989) talk about the serious limitations in social skills progress in preschool children with autism that result from "their failure to generalize" (p. 356). These authors distinguish between the following two different types of generalization:

> Most typically social behavior learned in one setting does not occur in other settings. Skills learned in the presence of certain children or adults are not used in the presence of other people. Behavior learned at one time seems lost or forgotten a short time later if the exact conditions of training are not present. All of these are examples of failures in stimulus generalization. Response generalization is a similar, difficult problem. A student may learn one response and use it consistently, but when a somewhat different response is called for, generalization does not occur. [p. 356]

Berkell (1992) echoes the sentiments of Olley and Stevenson, and makes a strong case for the link between generalization and learning, "Generalization strategies, including teaching skills across settings, materials, and people, are *crucial to successful instruction*" (italics added; p. 101). Likewise, Klin and Volkmar (2000) list the following as one of six specifications felt to be "positive and necessary" when judging the appropriateness of programming for students with Asperger syndrome: "An important priority in the program is to foster generalization of learned strategies and social skills. . . . From a programming perspective what is important is to define generalization explicitly as a goal to be achieved, including the various specific strategies to be implemented and the goals in the light of which the success of the program will be measured" (p. 348).

The bottom line when it comes to generalization is that there is clear research evidence that demonstrates that the success of the student's educational program is directly linked to the degree to which he or she has achieved generalization of acquired skills across settings, people, and activities. We think that Powers (1992) put it best when he said, "The powerful instructional technologies that have been developed over the years will be of little long-term value to children with autism [or to children with other disabilities] if skills acquired fail to generalize to untrained environments" (p. 237). Clearly, while the generalization needs are not as well documented in the research literature for students with conditions other than ASD, there is ample anecdotal information that indicates that these students will, nonetheless, be well-served by greater attention to generalization of skills. Therefore, we believe that for all of these students, and for the population of children with autism in particular, generalization strategies and conditions should be expressed in the IEP, and directly addressed, if the goal of appropriateness is to be realized.

If this information is insufficient to convince skeptics of the importance of direct attention to generalization, consider the federal court case *Drew P. v. Clarke County School District* (1989). In this case the lack of generalization of skills from the school environment to the home was cited as a material reason why the child's parents withdrew their son from the public school and placed him in a private residential program for students with autism. The court, applying the *Rowley* standard (*Board of Education v. Rowley,* 1982), decided in favor of the parents that this placement was necessary in order for the student to derive any educational benefit.

We have spent a good deal of time on the issue of generalization in order to make the case for careful attention to it; however, our interpretation of how the concept of generalization dovetails with that of appropriate education, while informed by research and clinical practice, is ours alone. Nevertheless, our arguments in favor of including specific information on generalization in the IEP are made on sound educational grounds.

> *There is clear research evidence demonstrating that the success of the student's educational program is directly linked to the degree to which he or she has achieved generalization of acquired skills across settings, people, and activities.*

NUTS AND BOLTS

A mistake that teachers and clinicians make far too often is to treat generalization, quite literally, as an afterthought—something to be thought of *after* the student has acquired a particular skill. In many cases, that is too late. Remember the adage noted at the beginning of this chapter, "Begin with the end in mind" (Covey, 1989, p. 95). Specifically, given the profound difficulty that students with ASD have with the generalization of skills, it is necessary to begin this time- and labor-intensive process at the beginning of the teaching cycle, rather than at the end. Moreover, we consider this to be an excellent practice for all students with special needs, as well.

While it is beyond the scope of this book to provide detailed how-to information on generalization, members of the IEP team are encouraged to seek out information on the principles of generalization and the strategies that promote it. Hence, we refer the reader to the work of Stokes and Osnes (1988). For our purposes it is important to highlight four interrelated factors of which educators and clinicians need to be mindful as they set about the task of programming for generalization. First is *time*. Simply stated, students with special needs require a great deal of "time in" when it comes to skill development across different settings, activities, and people in order to have sufficient practice in these contexts. The second factor is *structured opportunities*. Mere exposure to different settings, activities, and people is not enough. Instead, the educator should *create* structured opportunities for the skills to occur in each of the targeted circumstances. The final two factors, while important for all students with special needs, are arguably the most important for students with ASD. Teachers and clinicians need not only *assist students in making the connections* that they may not be able to make for themselves but also *scaffold skill development* by providing the necessary supports.

> *Teachers and clinicians need not only to assist students in making the connections that they may not be able to make for themselves but also to scaffold skill development by providing the necessary supports.*

DOCUMENTING THE PROTOCOL

There are many ways to include generalization information in the IEP. The most direct way is to include it in the body of the annual goal and short-term objectives:

- Specify eight out of ten structured opportunities per week, across a minimum of three different people, activities, and settings.

- Specify comprehension of six concrete concepts across a minimum of three different settings, activities, and people each day until a consistency level of 80 percent for each concept is reached.

- Specify nine out of ten times, per story, across six different stories, and across a minimum of three different people and settings.

To avoid repetition, generalization criteria can also be specified as a "goal" in an addendum that is separate from the annual goal and short-term objectives. Consider the following:

> Generalization goal: *Seven to ten structured opportunities for practice will be provided across people, activities, and settings throughout the day until a performance level of 90 percent for each generalization target is reached.*

WRAPPING UP THE MAIN POINTS

- It is necessary to begin the time- and labor-intensive process of generalization of skills at the beginning of the teaching cycle rather than at the end.

- It is up to the IEP team to choose the particular manner in which to express generalization criteria—within annual goals and short-term objectives or within an addendum, although sometimes the format is dictated by the IEP form itself.

- It is strongly recommended that information about generalization be explicitly expressed in order to ensure attention to it and mastery of skills across people, settings, and activities.

- Maintenance of skills over time is intimately related to generalization. If there is no attention to the generalization of skills, and they are exhibited in only one activity and setting with one person— for example, with the speech-language pathologist in the therapy room—the student cannot maintain those skills.

- When students are able to make the connections that signal the need for newly acquired skills across various settings, activities, and people, they are far more likely to maintain the skills over time because the skills will be more functional and useful.

- We recommend that "mastered" skills be recycled across activities, environments, and people on a regular basis throughout the course of the year.

CHAPTER

7

GETTING TO THE HEART OF THE MATTER: HOW TO WRITE MEANINGFUL GOALS AND OBJECTIVES

"Without goals, and plans to reach them, you are like a ship that has set sail with no destination."

— Fitzhugh Dodson

Lest the reader wonder why we have waited until the seventh chapter of this book to finally get to the "heart" of the matter, please rest assured that we have done so by design. Specifically, we believe that annual goals and short-term objectives or benchmarks are so vital to the success of the student's educational program that they should be considered only after the IEP team has carefully reviewed the factors that are integral to their achievement. Toward this end, in the previous chapters we discussed the crucial building blocks of IEP development that are of central importance in constructing need-based, appropriate annual goals and short-term objectives: present levels of performance; underlying conditions; methodology; criteria and prompt levels; and generalization. We are now ready to apply the information we've already discussed to the writing of annual goals and short-term objectives. Before doing so, it is necessary to more fully discuss what is arguably the most consequential change in IDEA 2004: the controversial decision to require short-term objectives or benchmarks *only* for those students who receive alternate, as opposed to grade-level standard assessments. Later in this chapter we will define the distinction between short-term objectives and benchmarks and address the pitfalls to avoid when writing goals and objectives.

In what we believe was a gigantic step backwards, IDEA 2004 eliminated the requirement to include short-term objectives and benchmarks in the IEP except in cases where students are required to take alternate assessments. Here again, one sees deference to NCLB. Those in favor of this decision argued that it would minimize paperwork—a rationale that pales in comparison to its possible educational fallout. In the absence of short-term objectives or benchmarks—*the specific intent of which is to demarcate progress*—careful attention to progress can be compromised, as can one's ability to recognize, in a timely fashion, the parameters that signal the need for midcourse corrections. To be clear, although the particular method for gauging progress has been eliminated for some students, the actual requirement to determine and report progress has *not* been eliminated. Specifically, progress-reporting requirements are the same for children with disabilities as for nondisabled children. Therefore, progress must be assessed at least as often as every grading period. In our experience, nine- or six-week reporting periods are the most common.

What is particularly troubling about deciding to eliminate short-term objectives and benchmarks for students taking standard assessments is that this is in direct conflict with IDEA 2004's new emphasis on accountability because, clearly, the best and most efficient way to determine progress toward the goal is through short-term objectives or benchmarks. Without them, the likelihood of using more subjective standards for determining growth—such as teacher judgment or observation—increases. Furthermore, eliminating short-term objectives and benchmarks not only flies in the face of the intent of IDEA 2004 to increase accountability but also leaves school districts vulnerable to legal challenges. And most important, subjective reporting of progress is not in the best educational interests of students. Bateman and Herr (2006) summarize the issue succinctly: "A failure to include short-term objectives or benchmarks in *every* [italics added] IEP is short-sighted, legally risky, and very poor practice" (p. 12). We heartily agree with this opinion, and in fact recommend using one or the other of these important progress markers in *all* IEPs, regardless of the ill-conceived "pass" given by IDEA 2004 to students who receive grade-level standard assessments.

DISTINGUISHING BETWEEN SHORT-TERM OBJECTIVES, BENCHMARKS, AND GOALS

Short-term objectives are usually thought of as the intermediate steps toward the achievement of the annual goal; in contrast, benchmarks refer to the major milestones achieved during specific reporting cycles. Both help determine progress toward the annual goal.

According to the Florida Department of Education (2000), benchmarks and short-term objectives are similar in the following ways: "They provide a map or path the student will take to attain the annual goal. They link the preset level of educational performance and the annual goal. They guide the development of effective and relevant modifications and strategies" (p. 50).

Random House Webster's College Dictionary defines *goal* as "the result or achievement toward which effort is directed; aim; end" (Costello, 1991, p. 571). *Objective* is defined as "something that one's efforts or actions are intended to attain or accomplish; purpose; goal" (p. 933). Synonyms for both words are virtually identical. So how can they be distinguished from each other? In his book *The Complete IEP Guide: How to Advocate for Your Special Ed Child*, Lawrence M. Siegel (2001) looks at goals as broad statements of educational aims for students, and at objectives as "the skills [the] child must master to reach a stated goal" (p. 9/2). We agree with Siegel's subtle distinction between goals and objectives. Nevertheless, it is important to note that since the 2004 revisions to IDEA, goals have taken on greater specificity. Indeed, they have taken on many similarities to objectives as characterized by Siegel.

MEASURING SHORT-TERM OBJECTIVES, BENCHMARKS, AND GOALS

Under IDEA 2004, *measurability* is the standard-bearer for all three. Where there was some flexibility before the reauthorization of IDEA, in that measurability could be assigned to the objectives and benchmarks and not necessarily to the annual goal (Siegel, 2001), there is no such flexibility in IDEA 2004. Under the new requirements, the IEP must contain a statement of measurable annual goals—both academic and functional—as well as a description of how progress toward meeting them will be measured. In addition, the IDEA 2004 regulations also contain specific language requiring the IEP to specify the timing of periodic reports on the child's progress toward achievement of the annual goals. And in further deference to NCLB, the regulations tie periodic reporting on progress to the issuance of report cards for nondisabled students.

Although IDEA 2004 requires that goals be measurable in order to determine the amount of progress the student has made vis-à-vis his or her present levels of performance, it does not define *measurability*. This is of little concern when the skill areas are quantifiable—for example, being able to read all of the Dolch sight words in a given period of time. But measurability becomes much more difficult when the skill in question does not easily lend itself to quantitative measurement, as is the case for many of the goals presented in Part Two of this book. The issue of measurability will be discussed more fully in Chapter Eight.

Although IDEA 2004 requires that goals be measurable in order to determine the student's amount of progress, measurability is difficult when the skill in question does not easily lend itself to quantitative measurement.

Goals

The annual goal in the IEP is the statement of what the team hopes to accomplish in a given year for a given domain or area of instruction. Because IDEA 2004 requires that the goal be stated in measurable terms, it may be construed as the end product of a series of short-term objectives or benchmarks designed to move the student toward it. For example, if the goal is to teach the student to use four problem-solving strategies, then the three short-term objectives might cover the use of one problem-solving strategy (in the first objective), two (in the second objective), and three in the third objective, leading to the fourth "objective" (the use of four problem-solving strategies), which is actually the stated annual goal. It should be noted that the use of three short-term objectives fits nicely into the nine-week progress reporting cycle that many schools use.

Before we go further, it is important to consider a common problem in the statement of annual goals—that is, the use of "hedge" words, those that are vague or obfuscatory. This practice stems from confusing process with product or outcomes. Here are some hedge words: *develop an understanding of, develop an appreciation of, learn to recognize*. Clearly, each of these phrases is process- rather than outcome-oriented, because developing an understanding or appreciation of and learning to recognize are highly subjective behaviors that are cultivated over time and are resistant to objective analysis. The use of hedge words adds unnecessary layers that obfuscate overt performance (outcomes) and render objective judgment impossible. Instead of *develop an understanding or appreciation of,* it would be more to the point to say that the *student will choose the correct answer* (hence *demonstrating* understanding, rather than somehow *developing* it). If hedge words are used, there should be a description of the behaviors or outcomes that will be accepted as indicative of the phrase. So, for *understanding,* the description would be *selecting the correct answer*. Likewise, *learning to recognize* could be rewritten as *student will select.* This phrase points directly to the desired outcome—the act of identifying something, as opposed to the process of learning to do so.

Objectives

In the early days of P.L. 94–142, the forerunner to IDEA, instructional objectives were written with the thought, care, and respect they deserved. Fuzzy language, difficult-to-grasp abstractions, and impossible-to-measure requirements were considered unacceptable. After all, the mid-1970s belonged in large part to behaviorism, with its emphasis on observable outcomes and measurable performance. In those days the science of objective writing trumped the art of objective writing. With few exceptions, objectives were crisply worded and clearly stated. They also included the conditions for performance and the criteria by which to judge progress. The only real downside to all of this was the throw-the-baby-out-with-the-bathwater phenomenon. Specifically, in some cases, rigid adherence to the observable and measurable requirements for behavior led some individuals to disregard the instruction of important material simply because they weren't able to state objectives for it in observable or measurable terms. Nevertheless, the rule of the day was that objectives "said what they meant, and meant what they said."

But over time the IEP gradually came to reflect society's inexorable march toward greater permissiveness, and as such, was watered down. To wit, IDEA 2004 calls for short-term objectives to be eliminated altogether for students who take standard assessments. Even when short-term objectives are included in the IEP—as with students taking alternative assessments—they are often poorly stated or missing important elements. Take, for instance, the specification of underlying conditions. Once a mainstay of instructional objectives underlying conditions, today these specifications are often catch-as-catch-can or missing altogether. Likewise, notwithstanding the requirement for measurability that relies on *observable* behavior, many IEPs contain objectives that target behavior that is impossible to measure (as in *developing an appreciation for art*). Worse yet, percentages continue to be assigned arbitrarily, and in many cases, absurdly so. Consider the following example, taken from an actual IEP:

Mark will independently respect other people's needs, rights, and desires when asked—80%.

Even before one ponders what the 80 percent refers to, how to measure respect, or how to determine "people's needs, rights, and desires," the oxymoron (independently/when asked) renders the objective and its accomplishment moot! Unfortunately, when there are inadequate or inappropriate measurement standards for performance (not to mention impossible requirements), there is no accountability for results.

When goals and objectives are poorly stated or cannot be measured they stand in the way of appropriate educational programming and effective service delivery. Hence, IEP teams should take a hard look at student IEPs and ask the following question: *Does this IEP provide the necessary specifications to enable school staff to build appropriate educational programs, and deliver effective instructional services to students?* If the answer to this question is not an unqualified *yes*, then the information in this book can go a long way toward rectifying the situation.

THE IEP AS A SYSTEM OF INTERDEPENDENT COMPONENTS

Random House Webster's College Dictionary defines the term *system* as "an assemblage or combination of things or parts forming a complex or unitary whole" (Costello, 1991, p. 1356). The applicability of the term to the IEP is irrefutable. Consider the following. Annual goals and short-term objectives are the vehicles for delineating intended instructional outcomes. Hence, they are the means to a very important end—*appropriate education*. As important as objectives are, however, they do not stand alone. In fact, like the skeletal system in which one bone must connect to another for movement to become possible, so too the component parts of the IEP system must interconnect with one another for appropriate educational "movement" to take place. Consider how the following component parts fit together into a cohesive whole: (1) annual goals for students are derived on the basis of their priority educational needs expressed in the present levels of performance (PLP) statements; and (2) short-term objectives delineate the interim steps that move students toward the accomplishment of their annual goals. It should be obvious that if short shrift is given to either of these important components, the student's entire educational program will be at risk.

Another interdependent component of the IEP—and one that dovetails with the statement of annual goals and short-term objectives—is that of *methodology,* which was discussed in an earlier chapter. Robert F. Mager, an internationally renowned writer on training and education, and often considered the guru of instructional objectives, has this to say about the interrelationship between objectives and methodology: "When clearly defined objectives are lacking, there is no sound basis for the selection of instructional materials and procedures. If you don't know where you're going, how will you know which road to take to get there?" (Mager, 1997b, p. 14). Mager's logic is irrefutable. It makes the elimination of short-term objectives and benchmarks in the IEPs of students taking standard assessments all the more illogical, and it gives us yet another reason to argue for their continued use in all IEPs.

Short-term objectives, like annual goals, should be measurable because they are intimately connected to the criteria for performance. According to Mager (1997b), "Without clear objectives it simply isn't possible to decide which measuring instrument will tell you what you want to know" (p. 15). The remainder of this chapter will address the three essential features of sound objectives. Importantly, since IDEA 2004 has blurred the distinctions between goals and objectives that existed previously, the information on objectives clearly applies to the annual goals as well.

> *Short-term objectives, like annual goals, should be measurable because they are intimately connected to the criteria for performance.*

Objectives Must Be Useful

Throughout this book we have used the phrase *effective service delivery*, a phrase that is synonymous with appropriate instruction. Although all the essential elements of the IEP contribute to the effectiveness of instruction, it is the goals and objectives that "get the job done."

For instruction to be effective there must be a change in performance. If instruction merely maintains the status quo, it cannot be termed effective. Change, however, can go in either direction—it can result in desired gains or in undesirable outcomes. Needless to say, if instruction results in undesirable ends it is not only ineffective but also harmful. There are many ways in which objectives can be harmful. For example, goals and objectives that hold students to standards precluded by their disability not only prevent progress but also lead to frustration and anxiety. This usually occurs in situations where there is insufficient knowledge about the student's disability.

In order to avoid ineffective instruction or harmful side effects, it is also important to consider the characteristics of appropriate objectives. Mager (1997b) points out that for objectives to be appropriate they must be *useful*. As such:

- *Objectives must lead one to methodology that enables instruction to be "relevant and successful."*
- *Objectives must help "manage the instructional process itself."*
- *Objectives must lead one to the appropriate means for determining the extent to which instruction has been successful. [p. 43]*

Mager (1997b) also lists the following three characteristics that must be included in the body of the objective if it is to lead to effective instruction:

1. Performance: *describes what the learner is expected to be able to do.*
2. Conditions: *describe the circumstances under which performance is expected to occur.*
3. Criterion: *describes the level of competence that must be reached or surpassed. [p. 51]*

It should be clear that these same characteristics apply to the annual goals required by IDEA 2004. The underlying conditions for performance, as well as the criteria for it, have already been discussed in depth in previous chapters and need not be revisited here. Suffice it to say that they are intertwined not only with performance but also with all of the other essential elements of the IEP. Performance, however, does need further clarification.

Objectives Must Be Clear

Two performance issues are particularly crucial. The first and most obvious is that performance means *doing* something. Hence, if an objective is about *acting* on something, *selecting* the main idea, or *writing* a sentence, then what the learner has to do is obvious, because all of the italicized words are performatives that directly relate to observable behavior. But how does one handle performance based on behavior that cannot be directly observed? As noted earlier, some individuals have avoided this issue altogether, thus throwing the proverbial baby out with the bathwater. This is unacceptable, however, because the things that human beings value most in life are usually rooted in unmeasurables—such as truthfulness, responsibility, and so on. To dismiss them out of hand simply because they cannot easily be assessed is consummately short-sighted. Fortunately, Mager (1997a, 1997b) has a simple answer to this dilemma: he uses the term *indicator behavior* to represent actions or activities that can provide direct information when the objective is stated in covert terms. According to Mager (1997b), "We can write about covert performances in objectives [and goals] as long as there is a *direct* [italics added] way of finding out whether the performance is in good shape" (p. 77). The following examples clarify the intent of the covert wording:

> *Covert wording:* Discriminate shapes.

> *Indicator behavior:* Sort circles and squares (or triangles and rectangles, and so on).

> *Covert wording:* Understand verbs.

> *Indicator behavior:* Circle (or underline) verbs.

The best way to identify indicator behaviors is to ask oneself the question: *What does the student need to do to demonstrate mastery of the goal or objective?* (Mager, 1997a, 1997b). The list you generate will help you clarify overt performance.

It is important to note that there may be times when including the indicator behavior in the body of the annual goal or short-term objective is too cumbersome to be practical. At these times, it is acceptable to include the indicator behavior in an explanatory note. However you choose to do it, the bottom line is this: indicator behavior needs to be specified somewhere within the IEP document in cases where performance is covert.

Objectives Must Be Addressed in a Consistent Manner

Finally, we characterize *consistency* as covert only in the sense that it seems to simply emerge when the essential elements of the IEP interact to function as the well-oiled system it is designed to be. In fact, consistency is the crucial by-product of attention to all of the essential elements that lead to effective service delivery. Take, for example, the case of a child named Thomas and the differences between the following two objectives:

1. Thomas will develop an understanding of idioms.

2. Thomas will select from a group of four possible explanations the item that best describes what the idiom means.

Which of these two objectives has the better chance of being carried out in a consistent manner across people and activities? The answer to this question is obvious. The point to be made is that when objectives are clearly stated, comprehensive, and understandable, they are more apt to be carried out by a variety of people, across a variety of settings, and in the manner intended.

WRAPPING UP THE MAIN POINTS

- The IEP is a system of component parts in which each element must interconnect with one another in order for educational "movement" to take place.

- Properly worded goals and objectives must include information on *performance* (what is the student expected to be able to do?); *conditions* under which performance is expected to take place; and *criterion* for determining progress.

- When performance is covert, it is important to specify indicator behavior by which to judge progress.

- Three essential features of appropriate goals and objectives are that they must be useful, clearly stated, and addressed in a consistent manner by all persons.

CHAPTER

8

MEASURING STUDENT PERFORMANCE: MORE THAN A SIMPLE "NUMBERS GAME"

"You get what you measure. Measure the wrong thing and you get the wrong behaviors."

—*John H. Lingle*

Chapter Seven summarized how the essential elements of the IEP may be melded together into effective, functional, and measurable annual goals and short-term objectives. This chapter serves as a kind of "grand finale" to the process of designing effective IEPs, with its "Triple Crown" of *measurement, data collection*, and *evaluation*. In this chapter we consider the evaluation of the student's response to teaching methods, task expectations, and prompts and other supports, as well as a schedule for evaluation.

Unfortunately, many professionals find data collection, and all that it entails, formidable. After all, in this busy world of ours data collection involves paperwork, analysis, and interpretation—all of which are time-consuming. Moreover, many argue (with good reason) that data collection can be intrusive, interfering with the process of teaching, especially when working on functional skills in naturalistic contexts—for example, in a snack routine, where you might be up to your elbows in bananas! The problems of intrusion and interference are only compounded when you have to take data on multiple objectives across many different students. As a result, data collection is often haphazard, subjectively rendered (that is, based on teacher observation), and therefore consummately inadequate in measuring student progress. Several important issues will be discussed in the following sections of this chapter, each designed to address a question or concern about specific aspects of this important subject.

WHAT IS THE PURPOSE OF DATA COLLECTION?

On the surface, the answer to this question appears obvious. After all, most people understand that the main purpose of data collection is to determine students' progress toward achievement of their annual goals. That said, unless short-term objectives and benchmarks are clearly stated in measurable terms—not to mention actually used for *all* students—it will be very difficult to determine progress at periodic intervals throughout the year, as required by IDEA 2004. Hence, using measurable short-term objectives enables the IEP team to determine at appropriate reporting intervals

- The student's rate of learning

- The student's response to the methodology being used

- The student's response to prompts or cues and the extent to which these have been faded back to accommodate increased independence in skill development

- Whether the goal or objectives need to be revised as a result of early achievement, slower than expected progress, or other factors

- Whether there is adequate attention to the generalization of skills

Clearly, the collection of data on a regular basis yields critical information that is directly tied to student achievement. In fact, the information amassed from the collection of data serves as the fuel that drives clinical and educational decision making. Moreover, data collection at regular intervals ensures that such decision making is carried out in a timely manner, so that it may be used to make midcourse corrections in each of the areas noted in the bulleted list, if deemed necessary.

HOW OFTEN DOES DATA REALLY NEED TO BE TAKEN?

There is no simple, universal answer to this question. The timing of data collection depends on a variety of factors. In some cases, data collection may be methodology-driven. For example, in many discrete trial or applied behavior analysis (ABA) training programs, data collection is ongoing—it occurs at all times during the student's treatment sessions. In other treatment modalities, data collection is guided by the student's rate of learning. Thus, a more-able student with a higher rate of learning would be expected to progress more quickly, creating the need for relatively frequent data collection. Similarly, a less-able student with a slower rate of learning would likely require less frequent data collection. Here are some situational guidelines governing the frequency of data collection:

- *Methodology*: In general, the more structured the treatment session, the more frequently data collection may be expected to occur (discrete trial training). Conversely, when the setting is less structured (such as a community setting or other naturalistic context), data collection is generally less frequent.

- *Student's rate of learning*: As already stated, the faster a student progresses, the more frequently data collection needs to occur. A student who learns at a slower rate often requires less frequent data collection.

- *Demands of the learning situation*: In one-to-one situations, the demands on the instructor are often lower, allowing for more frequent data collection. More demanding situations (group lessons, community or naturalistic settings, and so on) require careful orchestration among teaching, monitoring, and data collection. In these situations, it is often more practical to take data at periodic intervals (that is, weekly or biweekly) throughout the year.

- *Frequency with which the goal or objective is addressed*: When a goal or objective is addressed frequently, such as every day, data may be taken on a daily or a more periodic basis, such as weekly. Objectives that are addressed less frequently, such as once per week, which may be the case in a speech or occupational therapy session, generally require data collection each time the objective is addressed, because contact with the student is limited.

- *Frequency with which the behavior is seen*: If a behavior is seen infrequently, it may be easy to keep a record of every instance in which it occurs. But if the behavior occurs frequently, the team may wish to use a time sampling procedure whereby data is taken during a specific time interval—one hour per day, five minutes per hour, and so on.

- *Type of data being collected*: Simple quantitative systems allow for easy and frequent data collection. Qualitative systems, however, may require a narrative description or subjective rating of performance. These factors add complexity to data collection, and require more time and effort. As a result, practicality may dictate that data be compiled on a less frequent basis.

These guidelines illustrate that there is a data collection spectrum, if you will, from high-frequency collection schedules to low-frequency schedules, against which the content of specific annual goals and short-term objectives may be evaluated to determine the best assessment schedule. Some of the more common data collection schedules found in IEPs are daily, weekly, biweekly, and monthly.

The bottom line on data collection schedules is that they need to fit the contours of the behavior addressed in the goal or objective and they need to be specified in the IEP document. Many school districts contain specific sections on their IEP forms for this purpose. When this is not the case, this information needs to be included in the body of the goal and objective.

The bottom line on data collection schedules is that they need to fit the contours of the behavior addressed in the goal and objective and they need to be specified in the IEP document.

WHEN IS QUANTITATIVE MEASUREMENT APPROPRIATE?

Quantitative measurement is not only the easiest type of data to collect and analyze but also the method of choice for most IEP teams. The main reason teams prefer this method over others is that quantification inspires a certain comfort level that other less precise data collection systems fail to provide. For one thing, quantitative data offers definitive information—you can determine at a glance whether the student has met (or is making progress toward) the goal. Usually, judgments on the quality of performance are unnecessary because there is a clear distinction between *correct* and *incorrect* (for example, Johnny has met his goal for reading all of the Dolch sight words).

Several means of quantitative measurement are available to IEP teams. Two of the most common methods are

- *Tally system*: The easiest form of quantitative measurement to use, this system involves a simple tally of correct and incorrect responses. Following collection, the percentage of correct responses is calculated. This type of system is best used with criteria that measure performance in percentages, specific numbers, or fractions.

- *Time measurement*: When criteria specify amount of time or a time-based fraction, time-based data may be gathered using a clock, stopwatch, finger count, or other method for recording this type of information.

Quantitative data may also be obtained using specific evaluation procedures that yield numerical scores. For example, a speech-language pathologist may specify as a criterion level a specific mean length of utterance (MLU; for example, 2.5). This MLU may be calculated quantitatively through the analysis of a language sample.

Unfortunately, there is a downside to this preference for quantitative data collection. Simply stated, sometimes (or even often!) it is applied in situations that do not lend themselves to quantification. Consider the following example:

Given cues, as needed, Heather will carry on a conversation with an adult or a peer—80%

One might ask what the 80 percent refers to: 80 percent of the time she spends with an adult or peer, or 80 percent of conversational accuracy (whatever that means!). Or, does it mean that she is required to engage in a conversation 80 percent of the time (leaving time for little else!)? The final question that should be asked is: Who's counting, anyway? In other words, quantitative data collection should not be used to assess behaviors that cannot (and should not) be quantified. Likewise, nonsensical percentages based on the alleged data should not be reported as evidence of progress.

WHEN IS QUALITATIVE MEASUREMENT APPROPRIATE?

Despite the appropriateness of quantitative measures for many of the types of behaviors that are commonly addressed in IEPs, some behaviors simply cannot and should not be addressed by quantitative means. This topic was addressed briefly in Chapter Five, but it deserves to be revisited here. Hence, at the risk of belaboring this very important point, as noted earlier, IDEA 2004 clearly requires that annual goals be measurable but it does not specify the means by which this should be accomplished. It should be obvious that the choice of the particular method of data collection is left up to the IEP team, and further, that this choice should be based on appropriateness and common sense. Lest the reader denigrate the use of qualitative measures as somehow inferior to quantitative measures, we offer the following as evidence of the usefulness of qualitative data: diagnosis of the syndrome of autism itself is made via qualitative as opposed to quantitative judgments of an individual's behavior. Furthermore, when one compares more-able students with ASD to their neurotypical peers, the most pronounced differences between the two are often seen in the subtle, qualitative ways in which those with ASD process information and express behavior. Clearly, what is needed here is an eclectic system of assessment that makes use of both quantitative and qualitative data, depending on the particular type of skill-related or behavioral information desired.

Because qualitative data is by nature subjective, a word of caution is in order. Judgments about the appropriateness of behavior are very much in the eye (or ear) of the beholder. In other words, there is often disagreement among members of the IEP team about the appropriateness of particular behaviors because standards for acceptable performance vary from person to person when there are no objective parameters by which to assess outcomes. In addition, behaviors that involve very subtle judgments lead to even greater confusion. The first step toward overcoming these difficulties is to be mindful of them, on the theory that to be forewarned is to be forearmed. Another is for the IEP team to take a few moments during the planning and placement team meeting to define what constitutes appropriateness for the behavior to be judged.

Despite the appropriateness of quantitative measures for many of the types of behaviors that are commonly addressed in IEPs, some behaviors simply cannot and should not be addressed by quantitative means.

Once the IEP team has clearly defined the behaviors that need to be measured, a system of data collection must be delineated. There are two primary means of analyzing qualitative aspects of behavior:

- *Rating scales*: A predetermined scale is created for the purpose of making qualitative judgments about a student's performance with respect to a particular behavior. The scale should contain enough information to ensure that a given behavior is judged in a similar manner by different raters. Rating scales provide a practical means of quantifying, if you will, the qualitative process of judging the appropriateness of the student's behavior. Consider the following rating scale, designed for use with a student diagnosed with a speech-language impairment who uses an inappropriate volume level when speaking:

  - *Level 1*: Student uses appropriate conversational volume (for example, individuals in close proximity to the student are not disrupted).

  - *Level 2*: Student's vocal volume is moderately high (individuals within a seven- to ten-foot radius are disrupted by the loudness of the student's voice).

  - *Level 3*: Student's vocal volume is excessively high (individuals at distances greater than ten feet are disrupted).

A similar scale can be designed for a student whose speech volume is too soft, or whose rate of speech is inappropriate. In addition, rating scales can be used for many other behaviors that require qualitative judgments

- *Narrative description*: This data collection method is often used to assess progress in such amorphous skill areas as social skills development, theory of mind, and problem solving. Narrative description may also be used to supplement quantitative measures, such as tallies, particularly when judgments regarding the quality of performance are desired. Consider the following example:

  Given prior review of problem-solving strategies, Philip will apply them to specific problems, or seek the assistance of others who can help him, in the vocational setting, four out of five opportunities, independently.

In this example, narrative description can provide an effective way to monitor the manner in which the student applies problem-solving strategies, as well as the timeliness and appropriateness with which he enlists (or fails to enlist) the help of others. Furthermore, an additional objective, stated in quantitative terms, could address the number of times the student was successful in solving the problem.

WRAPPING UP THE MAIN POINTS

- Measurability is not an option—it's a requirement. Whether quantitative or qualitative data collection measures should be used depends on the nature of the specific behavior to be measured.

- The use of narrative description is not without controversy because it is the method of data collection most open to interpretation.

- The flexibility in data collection that narrative description affords creates an even greater need for a clear and detailed definition of behavioral expectations when the IEP is being developed or reviewed.

- Clear definitions go a long way toward providing assurance that the narrator will observe, and therefore describe, the appropriate behavior.

CHAPTER 9

IN THE SHADOW OF NO CHILD LEFT BEHIND

"The wheel is come full circle."

—*William Shakespeare*

In this chapter we cover those elements in IDEA 2004 that, for our purposes, can be handled with a broader stroke: the least restrictive environment (LRE) provision; participation in state or districtwide assessments; the distinction between the terms modifications and accommodations; and related services and supplementary aids and services.

A "PLACE" CALLED LRE

As noted previously, the LRE provision did not change in IDEA 2004. Nevertheless, the case may be made that LRE has taken on even greater emphasis as a result of IDEA 2004's alignment with NCLB. Interestingly, although some of the IEP elements covered in the previous chapters were becoming watered-down in practice (neglecting to provide underlying conditions, for example), or worse yet, were going the way of the "scrap heap" by direct assertion in IDEA 2004 (allowing the elimination of short-term objectives and benchmarks for students who take standard assessments), the LRE provision was developing greater clout with each passing year. By the dawn of the new millennium, IDEA's *preference* for the least restrictive environment began to take on the properties of a *demand note*, paralleling the popularity of the inclusive education movement that began as a small snowball rolling down the hill in the mid-1980s, only to become a veritable avalanche by the end of the century.

The commitment to LRE was reinforced by NCLB, which was signed into law on January 8, 2002. This commitment has become so strong that many school districts across the country have abandoned their special education classrooms in deference to the inclusive classroom setting. Congress clearly paved the way for this in its attempt to ensure that "special education can become a service for such children [those with special needs] rather than a place where such children are sent" (Wright and Wright, 2006, p. 46). Despite the soundness of this reasoning, it is consummately ironic that, in many cases, LRE has become a *place* called the mainstream, rather than a *programmatic option* to be determined according to the needs of each individual student! According to Wright and Wright (2006), "Pursuant to the least restrictive environment requirement in Section 1412(a)(5), *special education services* [italics added] should be delivered in general education settings except 'when the nature or severity of the disability of the child is such that education in regular classes with the use of supplementary aids and services cannot be achieved satisfactorily'" (p. 46).

Although it is true that the requirement that children with disabilities be educated in the least restrictive environment is at the very core of IDEA 2004, and further, that access to the mainstream is an absolute right of students with disabilities, the issue of *appropriateness* seems to have gotten lost in the shuffle! In fact, we would argue that to determine the appropriate classroom setting for a student with special needs it is necessary to ask the following question: *Where does the student do his or her best learning?* If the answer is that the student learns best in a less complex, specialized environment, in which there are fewer students, fewer distractions, and many more opportunities to learn and practice the skills they will need to be successful, then that is the least restrictive environment in which the student can receive a free appropriate public education. Hence, we strongly believe that to honor a particular setting (the inclusive classroom) over the specific needs of the student is to glorify form over substance to the detriment of the student's educational success.

We feel that we are on secure legal (not to mention logical) grounds on the issue of LRE. We base this assertion on the fact that despite the preference for inclusion in IDEA 2004, it nonetheless recognizes that for some students with disabilities the inclusive classroom may *not* be the *least* restrictive environment in which they can derive educational benefit. Specifically, IDEA 2004 uses the qualifier "to the maximum extent appropriate" to confer a relative standard on LRE decisions that ties the determination of placement to the particular needs of the student. In addition, according to Siegel (2001):

- *First, LRE is really a characterization of a placement or program, not necessarily a specific place.*

- *Second, the LRE placement for a child is primarily the location of the program, but should also involve the programmatic components—for example, the size of the class, the kinds of children and the type of school. [p. 2/5]*

From the point of view of appropriateness and the best educational interests of the student, we think that Attorney Siegel is right on!

Before leaving the topic of LRE, we'd like to turn briefly to the subject of what to do when there is nowhere other than the mainstream in which to place the student. In other words, what's a parent to do when the school's commitment to LRE causes it to offer no option but the inclusive classroom setting for a student who needs a specialized environment? Clearly, from the perspective of the best educational interests of the student, this is unacceptable. It would also seem to be contrary to the intent of IDEA 2004, which mandates that schools build programs around students according to their individual needs, rather than fit students into programs—mainstream or otherwise—simply because they're "the only game in town." Support for this position comes from Wright and Wright (1999): "In all cases, placement decisions must be individually determined on the basis of each child's abilities and needs, and not solely on factors such as category of disability, significance of disability, availability of special education and related services, configuration of the service delivery system, availability of space, or administrative convenience" (p. 211).

> *To honor the inclusive classroom over the specific needs of the student is to glorify form over substance to the detriment of the student's educational success.*

STATE AND DISTRICTWIDE ASSESSMENTS

Nowhere do the IDEA 2004 requirements reflect NCLB requirements more closely than when discussing participation in assessments. According to the wording of the law: "All children with disabilities are included in *all* general state and districtwide *assessment programs,* including assessments described under Section 6311 of this title, with *appropriate accommodations and alternate assessments where necessary* and as indicated in their respective individualized education programs" (as cited in Wright and Wright, 2006, p. 80). Guidelines for appropriate accommodations have been developed by the state, or in the case of districtwide assessments, by the local education agency (LEA). There are also guidelines for participation in alternate assessments. Clearly, the alignment of IDEA 2004 and NCLB is perhaps most obvious in the language used to refer to accommodations and alternate assessments. To wit, IDEA 2004 *requires* that alternate assessments be "*aligned* with the State's challenging *academic content standards and* challenging student *academic achievement standards*" (as cited in Wright and Wright, 2006, p. 80). This requirement is most unfortunate because it is not based on, nor does it take into account, the individual needs of the student, but rather "tethers" the student's learning to curricular content that, while appropriate for typical students, is likely arbitrary or even inappropriate for those with significant special needs.

One last word of caution: in order for the IEP team to make the decision that a particular student must take an alternate assessment rather than participate in the standard state or districtwide assessment, it must document the following: (1) why the student is unable to participate in the standard assessment, and (2) why the alternate assessment that is selected for the student is appropriate

Nowhere do the IDEA 2004 requirements reflect NCLB requirements more closely than when discussing participation in assessments.

to his or her needs. Finally, as noted previously, the IEP must also include a description of short-term objectives or benchmarks for those students who fall under the alternate assessment requirement. We hope we have already made the case for including short-term objectives or benchmarks in the IEPs of *all* students.

ACCOMMODATIONS VERSUS MODIFICATIONS

Although the terms *accommodation* and *modification* are more often than not used interchangeably, there are important differences between them that have significant implications for students with disabilities. As the term *accommodation* implies, the emphasis is on assisting, aiding, or obliging the student so that he or she is more available for learning and able to derive benefit from the curriculum. This can be done by removing, to the extent possible, barriers to success, or by increasing the circumstances favorable to successful performance. Accommodations may be made with respect to instruction or assessment. For example, accommodations may be made to the following:

- Instructional methods, teaching style or delivery, and curricular materials

- Classroom and homework assignments

- Assessment tools and ways of responding

- Time requirements

- The environmental setting

- The manner and type of student output (for example, oral recitation or using a computer for fine-motor difficulty)

According to Twachtman-Cullen (2001, p. 10), "Accommodations refer to the adjustments that are made to ensure that the students with disabilities have both equal access to educational programming, and the means by which to demonstrate success. *Once accommodations are made, students with special needs are expected to meet the standards for all students*" [italics added]. It should

Although the terms accommodation *and* modification *are more often than not used interchangeably, there are important differences between them.*

be obvious from this that accommodations are not intended to create a different (lower) standard for students with disabilities, but rather to enable them to meet the expectations for all students. Basically, accommodations are intended to empower school personnel to do what it takes to "get around" the limitations imposed by the student's disability. As such, accommodations are especially important in the inclusive classroom setting, because they can spell the difference between success and failure for students with special needs. Indeed, accommodations in the form of supplementary aids and services *must* be provided in the regular education setting before a student with special needs can be removed from that setting to a more restrictive one. The following points are important:

- Accommodations are not limited to those areas mentioned in the preceding list, but are confined only by the boundaries of one's creativity and imagination.

- It is not only the responsibility but also the obligation of the school to accommodate the student with special needs.

- Accommodations should be thoroughly discussed by the IEP team and documented in the body of the IEP.

In contrast, it should be obvious that the term *modification* implies change. Hence, it is fundamentally different from that of *accommodation*. According to Twachtman-Cullen (2001, p.10), "Modifications . . . refer to substantive changes in course/subject delivery, content, or instructional level *that have the effect of creating a different standard for students with disabilities*" [italics added]. Although there may be some degree of overlap between the two terms, there is one critical difference: educational outcomes. In other words, unlike accommodations, modifications create a different (lower) standard of performance for students with special needs, whereby they are not expected to meet the curricular requirements and educational standards of regular education.

Modifications are generally made to the educational programs of students who are eligible for alternate assessments, because they have very different learning needs than their peers who participate in standard grade-level assessments. Furthermore, decisions about modifications are strictly within the purview of certified staff, as opposed to paraprofessional support staff, because they involve a lower academic standard. It is therefore vitally important that the IEP team discusses and clearly delineates what it intends with respect to modifications. Last but not least, it is also critically important that, like accommodations, modifications be documented in the IEP.

RELATED SERVICES AND SUPPLEMENTARY AIDS AND SERVICES

According to *Roadmap to IDEA 2004: IEPs, Highly Qualified Teachers, & Research Based Instruction* (Wrightslaw, 2010), the primary change to this section of IDEA 2004 is that related services and supplementary aids and services "be based on peer-reviewed research to the extent practicable." Clearly, this raises the bar on these elements of the IEP, while at the same time it holds school districts to a higher standard when it comes to evidence-based practices.

There is a good deal of confusion between what is meant by *related services* versus *supplementary aids and services*. According to Wright and Wright (2006), "Related services are services the child needs to benefit from special education" (p. 54). Speech-language pathology and occupational therapy services would be considered related services. IDEA 2004 defines supplementary aids and services as "aids, services, and other supports that are provided in regular education classes or other education-related settings, and in extracurricular and nonacademic settings, to enable children with disabilities to be educated with nondisabled children to the maximum extent appropriate" (as cited in Wright and Wright, 2006, p. 203).

WRAPPING UP THE MAIN POINTS

- The requirement that children with disabilities be educated in the least restrictive environment is at the very core of IDEA 2004, but the issue of *appropriateness* seems to have gotten lost in the shuffle.

- To determine the appropriate classroom setting it is necessary to ask the question: *Where does the student do his or her best learning?* If the student learns best in a specialized environment, then that is the least restrictive environment in which the student can receive a free appropriate public education.

- Part One of this book covered the essential elements of the IEP. A comprehensive understanding of them will enable IEP teams to design annual goals and short-term objectives or benchmarks for core academic areas or ancillary domains of functioning that are individualized to the student's needs and comprehensible to all those responsible for carrying them out.

- This volume concentrates on cognitive and social-cognitive areas of functioning rather than on academic goals and objectives because (1) these areas of development are both supportive of, and critical to academic success, (2) students with the conditions discussed in this book have specific impairments in many areas of cognitive and social-cognitive functioning, and (3) IEPs are often sorely lacking in annual goals to address these areas of development.

Moving from Theory to Practice

10

TOOLS FOR ASSESSMENT AND DECISION MAKING

"Everything that can be counted does not necessarily count; everything that counts cannot necessarily be counted."

—*Albert Einstein*

Having discussed the essential elements of the IEP in terms of the intent of IDEA 2004 in Part One of the book, it is now time to translate the law's intent into practical application. Because this is often easier said than done, as our examples of poor practice illustrate, in this chapter we attempt to provide guidelines for bridging the gap between theory (the law) and practice (designing effective IEPs). This chapter also offers readers a "guided tour" through the remaining chapters of the book.

We consider the following to be prerequisites for writing appropriate, individualized, and measurable annual goals and short-term objectives that lead to effective educational service delivery:

- A comprehensive understanding of the essential elements of the IEP

- Adequate research-based knowledge about the student's disability and how it affects academic and functional performance

- Assessment information on the student's unique strengths, weaknesses, and needs across the specific areas of functioning affected by the disability

- A means for determining the student's priority educational needs for the coming year

- Knowledge of research-based methodology

As noted earlier, it is well beyond the scope of this book to provide disability-specific information or specific research-based methods to address student needs, but references for several excellent resources that address issues related to these topics may be found in Appendix B.

ASSESSING APPROPRIATELY

Because determining a student's strengths and weaknesses is integral to writing appropriate annual goals and short-term objectives, it is important to consider a few points about assessment. Although standardized assessment procedures are clearly preferable for determining level of functioning in some skill areas, they are not always appropriate (or even available) for many of the skill areas addressed in this book (for example, theory of mind). In such cases, one must consider other options, some of which will be discussed here.

Another consideration in assessment is that for many students with disabilities, *knowledge* does not always equal *application.* For example, a student with anger-management issues may be able to recite exactly what to do in an anger-provoking situation but may not be able to apply those strategies in the heat of the moment. Likewise, a child with an anxiety disorder may be able to skillfully describe how to solve the problems presented on a formal test of problem solving, thus achieving a test score within normal limits, yet evidence very poor problem-solving skills when highly stressed in a real-world situation.

> *Although standardized assessment procedures are clearly preferable for determining level of functioning in some skill areas, they are not always appropriate for many of the skill areas addressed in this book.*

In recent years, several excellent informal assessment instruments have been designed to capture hard-to-measure skills within the domains of functional communication and social interaction. One such example is the *Autism Diagnostic*

Observation Schedule (ADOS; Lord, Rutter, DiLavore, and Risi, 2002). This instrument involves the administration of several tasks and the subsequent coding of behaviors in categories such as *shared enjoyment in interaction, conversation,* and *coordination of eye contact with other means of communication.* Although the ADOS was originally designed as a tool to aid in the diagnosis of ASD—because it provides an excellent measure of functional communication—it can also be used to measure progress in communication and social areas for individuals with other disabilities. Executive function skills can also be measured using rating scales. One instrument to measure functional performance is the *Behavior Rating Inventory of Executive Function (BRIEF*; Gioia, Isquith, Guy, and Kenworthy, 2000). This scale, which has both parent and teacher versions, can measure eight individual executive functions. Hence, it not only can identify specific areas of need but also can measure functional progress within the subscale.

We'd like to caution the reader here against becoming an "assessment snob"—preferring *only* norm-based or formal assessment measures. For one thing, multidimensional skills such as those subsumed under the rubric of pragmatic communication, or those involved in theory of mind, do not lend themselves to static, one-dimensional formal assessment. For another, for some skills, formal measures may actually obfuscate, rather than clarify deficits. For example, many children with ASD score well on tests of word retrieval such as the *Expressive One-Word Picture Vocabulary Test (EOWPVT),* only to have significant word-retrieval problems in the heat of the cognitively demanding moment in a conversational exchange. Hence, reliance on the *EOWPVT* test score would mask the students' functional word retrieval difficulty. Indeed, formal assessment may not even be possible for students at the less able end of the autism spectrum continuum or for those with significant cognitive challenges stemming from other conditions. In such cases, informal assessment is usually the only reasonable way to determine functional performance.

Before leaving this topic, let's consider the concept of *dynamic assessment,* a term coined by Vygotsky in his classic book *Mind in Society* (1978). It has particular relevance for multidimensional areas of impairment such as pragmatics, theory of mind, and EF. Unlike traditional, context-free assessments that measure fully developed (all or nothing) competencies, dynamic assessment takes into account contextual elements in determining the *level* of (ongoing) skill development (Bodrova and Leong, 2007). By focusing on the level of skill development, one gains information about the degree of assistance the student needs and also the amount of progress he or she is making *toward* independent performance. This type of assessment seems better suited to the evaluation of complex, multifaceted skills. Furthermore, it captures the essence of the way in which the short-term objectives progress from greater to lesser assistance toward the accomplishment of the annual goal.

To summarize, all things considered (especially the *individualized* needs of the student!), use of a variety of assessment measures ranging from formal to informal, and including dynamic assessment procedures, are likely to give a more accurate and comprehensive picture of a student's functioning level and his or her functional performance in more complex, multifaceted domains. Finally, we advocate that educators and clinicians view all assessment as a dynamic and ongoing process, and also that they be mindful of the ways in which severe cognitive and social-cognitive challenges can compromise the assessment process and cloud test results.

DETERMINING PRIORITY EDUCATIONAL NEEDS

In cases of mild disability it may be possible to design annual goals and short-term objectives for all of the deficit areas requiring attention; however, in most cases, this is not possible because of the number of problem areas that require remediation. Because the IEP is intended to address the goals and objectives that the school hopes to accomplish in a given year—hence the term *annual* goals—an important part of IEP decision making requires that teams prioritize those areas of functioning that need immediate redress, putting others on temporary hold. In some cases, the process of establishing priorities is relatively easy. This is particularly true when dealing with behaviors that pose a danger to the student or his or her classmates, because such behaviors, by their very nature, demand immediate attention. Most of the time, however, the task of determining priority educational needs is more an art form than a scientific endeavor.

The following general guidelines will help IEP teams determine the priority educational needs that will serve as the foundation for the annual goals and short-term objectives for students:

- *Be logical!* Select early-developing behaviors and skills first.

- *Be sensible!* Select behaviors and skills that the student has a reasonable chance of learning in a year.

- *Be wise!* Select behaviors and skills that will make a significant and meaningful difference in the student's life.

Operating according to these guidelines isn't rocket science, as the saying goes. What it is, however—and what may be in shorter supply than rocket science—is common sense, an appreciation for developmental considerations, and sensitivity to the role of functionality and relevance in the lives of students with disabilities. Form 10.1, Priority Educational Need Analysis, provides the reader with a systematic approach for establishing priority educational needs on which to base annual goals. This user-friendly rating scale takes into account the following parameters:

- Severity

- Frequency

- Functionality/Relevance

- Developmental readiness

- Importance (of the goal) to the family

ATTENDING TO THE IEP ESSENTIAL ELEMENTS

It should be eminently clear by now that the essential elements of the IEP found in IDEA 2004 and covered in Part One are critical to appropriate education and effective service delivery. We now offer Form 10.2, The IEP Essential Elements Checklist. This form is intended to fulfill two important functions:

- Serve as a reminder for IEP teams to attend to all of the important elements of the IEP, even those that they might, otherwise, be tempted to leave to chance.

- Help promote accountability in overall IEP development.

OVERVIEW OF REMAINING CHAPTERS

The following five chapters of the book are our attempt to translate theory into practice. Hence, we take the information presented in Part One and apply it to the actual practice of writing annual goals and short-term objectives for students with ASD, ADD/ADHD, NLD, S/LI, and ED. Our aim in these chapters is twofold:

- To illustrate how the essential elements of the IEP may be melded together to generate measurable annual goals and short-term objectives for students with these conditions

- To provide examples of annual goals and short-term objectives for those areas of functioning that are typically impaired in students with the conditions covered in this volume, and which are often given short shrift in IEPs

FORM 10.1 PRIORITY EDUCATIONAL NEED ANALYSIS

Student's Name: _____ DOB: _____

Subject Area/Domain: _____ IEP dated from: _____ to _____

Proposed Annual Goal: _____

Rate the proposed annual goal along the parameters specified by circling the number that best applies. When finished, add the numbers and divide by 5 to determine the Educational Need Composite Score. Compare this score to those for other proposed annual goals for the purpose of determining whether or not there exists a priority educational need. This worksheet is not designed to replace sound clinical judgment. Rather, it is designed to help facilitate need prioritization.

A.	Severity					
Mild difficulty	1	2	3	4	5	Severe difficulty

B.	Frequency					
Infrequently required skill/behavior	1	2	3	4	5	Frequently required skill/behavior

C.	Functionality/Relevance					
Nonfunctional/Nonrelevant	1	2	3	4	5	Functional/Relevant

D.	Developmental Readiness					
Late developing skill/Prerequisites not yet mastered	1	2	3	4	5	Early developing skill/Prerequisites mastered

E.	Importance to Family					
Unimportant	1	2	3	4	5	Very important

Results: _____

Sum of Ratings: _____ / 5 = Educational Need Composite Score: _____

Priority Need Analysis (for example, Low, Moderate, High): _____

FORM 10.2 IEP ESSENTIAL ELEMENTS CHECKLIST

☐ Does the IEP contain a statement regarding the student's present level of academic achievement and functional performance?

☐ Are the present levels of performance statements sufficiently informative to serve as the basis for generating annual goals, as well as the standards by which to judge progress?

☐ Do the present levels of performance statements address how the student's disability affects his or her involvement and progress in the general education curriculum, or in the case of preschool students participation in appropriate activities?

☐ Are the underlying conditions clearly delineated for each short-term objective or benchmark and, where appropriate, for the annual goal?

☐ Is there sufficient information to determine the soundness of the methodology or procedures used and, to the extent possible, whether they stem from relevant research?

☐ Are the criteria for annual goals and short-term objectives or benchmarks meaningful, appropriate, and sufficient to permit judgment of performance?

☐ Are evaluation/data-collection procedures meaningful and appropriate to the annual goal and short-term objectives?

☐ Are evaluation/data-collection procedures tied to specific, periodic reporting intervals that are the same as those for nondisabled peers?

☐ Are prompt levels specified, and is there ongoing attention to the systematic fading back of prompts over time?

☐ Is there evidence of attention to the generalization and maintenance of skills?

☐ Do the long-term annual goals follow from the present levels of performance, and are they well-stated, measurable, and capable of being accomplished in a year?

FORM 10.2 (*continued*)

☐   Do the short-term objectives proceed logically to the annual goals, and are they meaningful, clearly stated, and measurable?

☐   Has the student been placed in the least restrictive environment in which he or she can make progress (with accommodations and supports) toward meeting the short-term objectives and annual goals?

☐   Are the necessary accommodations and supports in place to allow the student to function in the least restrictive environment and in extracurricular activities, and are they specifically documented in the IEP?

☐   Are all related services and supplementary aids and services clearly specified in the IEP?

☐   Does the IEP reflect the student's priority educational needs for the coming year?

☐   Is the IEP reasonably calculated to deliver appropriate educational programming?

Each of the next five chapters is devoted to a specific area of functioning, and each contains sample annual-goal and short-term-objective templates corresponding to subcategories within the general content area. Each chapter includes the same elements:

- A brief description of and rationale for our decision to include the content area for the disabilities addressed

- A list delineating the specific type of information required in the present levels of performance (PLP)

- The content areas covered in the chapter

- Sample PLPs and sample annual-goal and short-term-objective templates that IEP teams can adjust or build from to design their own individualized goals and objectives for students in their care

We use the term *template* to underscore that the sample annual goals and short-term objectives are offered *only* to demonstrate how the internal elements of each fit together, and how each objective systematically leads to the annual goal. In keeping with the critical importance of individualization, we do not offer the sample goals and objectives as finished products to be indiscriminately applied to students who manifest the deficit areas covered by them. Having said that, if after taking into account the individual needs of specific students it is found that particular goals and objectives, as written, do apply, by all means use them. In most cases, however, it will be necessary to adjust criterion and prompt levels, as well as specific content to suit individual needs and circumstances. Hence, the reader should construe the sample annual-goal and short-term-objective templates as the "builder's models" discussed in the construction metaphor in the Introduction. Moreover, in keeping with the generic nature of these templates, we use the impersonal designation *student,* in place of an actual name. Finally, although useful teaching resources for each of the content areas addressed in Part Two may be found in Appendix B, we have included *general teaching tips and strategies,* consisting of a potpourri of ideas, delivered in "stream of consciousness" fashion in each of the next five chapters.

WRAPPING UP THE MAIN POINTS

- The information and forms presented in this chapter will help streamline the decision-making process and enable IEP teams to more systematically address the essential elements of IEP development.

- The remaining chapters in this book will apply what we have discussed so far to designing annual goals and short-term objectives that meet the letter and spirit of IDEA 2004 and deliver appropriate educational services to students with ASD, ADD/ADHD, NLD, S/LI, and ED.

CHAPTER

11

COMPREHENSION: THE POWER THAT FUELS EXPRESSION

"Whatever you cannot understand, you cannot possess."

—*Johann Wolfgang von Goethe*

RATIONALE FOR INCLUDING SKILL CATEGORY

- Comprehension is the power that fuels language expression, and as such, comprehension precedes meaningful production in both typical children and those with developmental disabilities (Sevcik and Romski, 1997). In addition, pragmatic deficits occur on both a receptive and an expressive level (Twachtman-Cullen, 2000c).

- Research demonstrates that comprehension and concept development are areas of difficulty in students with ASD (Goldstein, Minshew, and Siegel, 1994; Minshew, Goldstein, Taylor, and Siegel, 1994); ADD/ADHD (Rief, 2005); NLD (Tanguay, 2001); and of course, in some students with S/LI.

- Difficulty comprehending nonverbal cues and signals is the core deficit in students with NLD, and also significantly problematic in students with ASD (Landa, 2000; Mundy and Sigman, 1989; Tantum, 2000).

PRESENT LEVELS OF PERFORMANCE FOR COMPREHENSION

The PLP for comprehension should include

- A statement indicating the student's strengths in comprehension skills, particularly as they relate to academic achievement and functional performance

- A statement about the student's weaknesses in specific areas of comprehension, particularly as they relate to academic achievement, functional performance, and priority educational needs for the coming year

- A statement on how the student's disability in comprehension affects his or her involvement and progress in the general curriculum (or for preschool children, in appropriate activities)

- The sources of the statements in the PLP (optional)

- Any additional information that can enable the PLP to fulfill its two important functions: (1) to serve as the basis for generating need-based, individualized IEP goals and objectives, and (2) to serve as the standard by which to judge student performance and progress

CONTENT AREA: CONCEPT DEVELOPMENT

Comprehending Concrete Concepts

Sample PLP for a six-year-old student with severe autism and cognitive impairment: Student presents with receptive language skills that are consistent with those of a two-year-old child, based upon observational data and parent report. While he demonstrates comprehension of several core concepts, on the basis of their function (that is, he knows how to use a whistle, cup, sock, and shoe), he does not yet know them as object labels (that is, he is not able to identify them when asked). Student's severe deficits in the comprehension of concrete concepts impede his ability to participate effectively in modified center-based programming, and severely limit his ability to play alongside or interact with peers.

Goal/Objective Templates Based on the PLP

Short-Term Objective 1:   Given direct teaching, repetition, and accompanying manual signs, student will demonstrate comprehension of 4 concrete concepts by responding appropriately to directives/comments regarding them in contextually relevant activities, 4/5 opportunities, across a minimum of 3 different activities and people, with hand-over-hand assistance, as needed.

Short-Term Objective 2: Given multisensory experiences with objects and accompanying manual signs, student will demonstrate comprehension of 2 additional concrete concepts, and maintenance of the 4 previously learned, by responding appropriately to directives/comments regarding them in contextually relevant activities, 4/5 opportunities, across a minimum of 3 different activities and people, with direct verbal and gestural cues.

Short-Term Objective 3: Given multisensory experiences with objects and accompanying manual signs, student will demonstrate comprehension of 2 additional concrete concepts, and maintenance of the 6 previously learned, by responding appropriately to directives/comments regarding them in contextually relevant activities, 4/5 opportunities, across a minimum of 3 different activities and people, given gestural cues.

Annual Goal: Student will demonstrate comprehension of 10 concrete concepts by responding appropriately to directives/comments regarding them 4/5 opportunities, across all settings, activities, and people, given expectant waiting.

Comprehending Abstract Concepts

Sample PLP for a four-year-old student with S/LI: Student demonstrates understanding of many core and concrete concepts that serve her well in her preschool classroom. She has a great deal of difficulty with abstract, relational concepts (for example, prepositions). Student's confusion over prepositions makes it difficult for her to follow directions in many academic learning tasks and in functional activities in her preschool inclusive classroom.

Goal/Objective Templates Based on PLP

Short-Term Objective 1: Given direct instruction and manual signs to accompany verbal directives, student will demonstrate comprehension of 4 prepositions by responding appropriately to directives in contextually appropriate activities and situations, 7/10 opportunities, across a minimum of 3 different settings, activities, and people, given direct verbal and gestural cues.

Short-Term Objective 2: Given manual signs to accompany verbal directives, student will demonstrate comprehension of 2 additional prepositions and maintenance of the previous 4, by responding appropriately to directives in contextually appropriate activities and situations, 8/10 opportunities, across a minimum of 3 different settings, activities, and people, given indirect verbal cues.

Short-Term Objective 3:　Given verbal directives, student will demonstrate comprehension of 2 additional prepositions and maintenance of the previous 6 by responding appropriately to directives in contextually appropriate activities and situations, 8/10 opportunities across a minimum of 3 different settings, activities, and people, given indirect verbal cues/expectant waiting.

Annual Goal:　Student will demonstrate comprehension of 8 prepositions by responding appropriately to directives involving them in contextually appropriate activities and situations, 9/10 opportunities across settings, activities, and people, independently.

CONTENT AREA: VERBAL LANGUAGE/INFORMATION PROCESSING

Comprehending Verbal Directions

Sample PLP for a five-year-old student with severe autism and cognitive impairment: According to observation and performance on both the *Peabody Picture Vocabulary Test (PPVT)* and the *Comprehensive Assessment of Spoken Language (CASL),* receptive language skills cluster in the 18–24 month range. While student has demonstrated comprehension of several one-step directions when presented in context with accompanying manual signs (for example, "sit down," "come here," and "stand up"), he is not always consistent in doing so. These difficulties affect his ability both to follow directions in academic tasks and to participate fully in day-to-day activities with peers in his preschool classroom.

Goal/Objective Templates Based on PLP

Short-Term Objective 1:　Given direct instruction, and manual signs to accompany verbal directives, student will demonstrate comprehension of 3 new one-step directions in contextually relevant activities, 7/10 opportunities, across a minimum of 3 different activities, settings, and people, given 2 repetitions of directions and physical assistance.

Short-Term Objective 2:　Given manual signs to accompany verbal directives, student will demonstrate comprehension of 2 additional one-step directions, and maintenance of the previous 3, in contextually relevant activities, 8/10 opportunities, across a minimum of 3 different activities, settings, and people, given 2 repetitions of directions and gestural cues.

Short-Term Objective 3:　Given manual signs to accompany verbal directives, student will demonstrate comprehension of 3 additional one-step directions, and maintenance of the previous 5, in contextually relevant activities, 8/10 opportunities, across a minimum of 3 different activities, settings, and people, given a maximum of 1 repetition and indirect verbal cues or expectant waiting.

Annual Goal: Given manual signs to accompany verbal directives, student will demonstrate comprehension of 10 one-step directions in contextually relevant classroom activities, 9/10 opportunities, independently.

Explanatory Notes:

- Accompanying manual signs aid the processing of verbal information, which is particularly important for students with ASD because they usually exhibit stronger skills in the visual (as opposed to auditory) domain. In the goal and objectives described above, manual signs paired with verbal directives give the student an additional input channel, and hence serve as the underlying condition for performance. Therefore, it is important to bear in mind that when manual signs are used in this manner—as an accommodation to aid auditory processing—they should not be faded out over time unless probes of the student's performance in the absence of manual signs indicate that it is safe to do so.

- Use of the phrase *will demonstrate comprehension* is tied to the action performed by the student to *demonstrate* that he or she has understood the task. In the preceding goal and objectives, it should be obvious that the action called for is that of carrying out the directives.

Processing Complex Information

Sample PLP for a fifteen-year-old student with S/LI: Student's comprehension skills serve her well in one-on-one and small-group situations (for example, the resource room/therapy room), according to both her teacher and speech-language pathologist. She has difficulty, however, comprehending verbal language as sentence length and complexity increase, as her performance on the *Clinical Evaluation of Language Fundamentals, Fourth Edition (CELF-4)* indicates. These difficulties negatively affect both her participation in academic activities and her grades overall.

Goal/Objective Templates Based on PLP

Short-Term Objective 1:   Given pre-teaching and a teacher-generated outline for 1 academic subject, student will demonstrate comprehension of verbal language by answering 3 questions appropriately in the resource/therapy room, 4/5 opportunities, given direct verbal cues.

Short-Term Objective 2:   Given teacher-generated outlines for 3 academic subjects, student will demonstrate comprehension of verbal language by answering 3 questions for each subject appropriately in the resource/therapy room, 4/5 opportunities, given indirect verbal cues.

Short-Term Objective 3:   Given teacher-generated outlines, student will demonstrate comprehension of verbal language by answering 3 questions appropriately across inclusive classroom settings for 2 academic subjects, 4/5 opportunities, given indirect verbal cues and manual sign prompts to refer to outline.

Annual Goal: Given teacher-generated outlines, student will demonstrate comprehension of verbal language by answering a minimum of 3 questions about the material within inclusive settings across 4 academic subjects, 4/5 opportunities, given gestural cues to refer to outline, as needed.

Comprehending Figurative Language

Sample PLP for a twelve-year-old student with NLD: Student's comprehension of language is quite good at the literal level, particularly when answering factual questions, according to his teacher, and as documented in formal testing. He has a great deal of difficulty with idiomatic expressions and figurative language, in general, which interferes with overall comprehension. His teacher reports that lately, student has become the target of ridicule by some of his classmates because of his literalness and lack of appreciation of jokes. These problems interfere with academic functioning in English and history classes, and with functional performance in nonacademic settings.

Goal/Objective Templates Based on PLP

Short-Term Objective 1:   Given direct instruction in the meaning of selected figures of speech, student will demonstrate comprehension of 10 idiomatic expressions by giving the literal definition when presented in isolation, with 80% accuracy given direct verbal cues.

Short-Term Objective 2:   Given a series of vignettes, student will demonstrate comprehension of 10 idiomatic expressions embedded in context by responding appropriately to them (that is, not taking them literally) in a variety of structured role-plays, with 80% accuracy, given indirect verbal cues.

Short-Term Objective 3:   Given a series of vignettes, student will demonstrate comprehension of 5 new idiomatic expressions, and maintenance of the previous 10 embedded in context, by responding appropriately to them in a variety of structured role-plays, with 80% accuracy, given expectant time delay, as needed.

Annual Goal: Given 15 familiar idioms embedded in contrived, real-world contexts, student will demonstrate comprehension by responding appropriately to them across academic settings, activities, and people, 4/5 opportunities, independently.

Understanding the Multiple Meanings of Words

Sample PLP for a ten-year-old student with high-functioning autism: Student manifests strengths in spelling, and in using vocabulary in a straightforward, literal manner. He has significant difficulty, however, understanding words when they are used in ways that are unexpected. For example, when a story character was defined as having *fair* hair, student became upset, saying, "But they weren't being fair!" The student's problem in understanding the multiple meaning of common words affects his interaction with peers, and makes it difficult for him to process information in a timely fashion in his fifth-grade inclusive classroom setting.

Goal/Objective Templates Based on PLP

Short-Term Objective 1: Given prior direct instruction, a set of cards containing 5 words with accompanying definitions that have multiple meanings (for example, train, play, and so on), and scenarios depicting 2–3 different uses for each word presented, student will demonstrate comprehension of multiple meanings by selecting the word/definition that matches each of the multiple-meaning scenarios, with 80% accuracy, given direct verbal and gestural cues.

Short-Term Objective 2: Given a set of cards containing 10 new and 5 previously learned words/definitions that have multiple meanings, and scenarios depicting 2–3 different uses for each word presented, student will demonstrate comprehension of multiple meanings by verbally supplying the word/definition that matches each of the scenarios, with 80% accuracy, given indirect verbal or gestural cues.

Short-Term Objective 3: Given a set of cards containing 5 new and 15 previously learned words/definitions that have multiple meanings, and scenarios depicting 2–3 different uses for each word presented, student will demonstrate comprehension of multiple meanings by verbally supplying the word/definition that matches each of the scenarios, with 80% accuracy, given expectant waiting.

Annual Goal: Given 20 previously learned words with multiple meanings, student will demonstrate comprehension of their contextually appropriate intended meanings by responding appropriately to them in contrived situations across academic and functional activities, with 90% accuracy, independently.

Understanding Story Narratives

Sample PLP for a nine-year-old student with Asperger syndrome: Student's strengths in narrative comprehension lie in her ability to remember the details of stories, many of which are irrelevant to the storyline. While she is able to answer general questions on what the story is about, she has significant difficulty identifying the main character, setting, and problem. Student's narrative comprehension difficulty affects her ability to perform adequately in all areas of the curriculum that involve an understanding of narrative information (for example, reading, language arts, social studies, and so on). It also affects her ability to work in a group with peers.

Goal/Objective Templates Based on PLP

Short-Term Objective 1: Given direct instruction in the use of a color-coded storyboard, student will demonstrate comprehension of main characters, setting, and problem by selecting pictures appropriate to the storyline from groups of 3 options, for use in telling about targeted story elements across 3 different stories, with 80% accuracy for each element, given direct verbal cues as needed.

Short-Term Objective 2: Given the use of a color-coded storyboard, student will demonstrate comprehension of main characters, setting, and problem by selecting pictures appropriate to the storyline from groups of 5 options, for use in telling about targeted story elements across 5 different stories, with 80% accuracy for each element, given indirect verbal cues as needed.

Short-Term Objective 3: Given a story read aloud by the teacher, student will demonstrate comprehension of main characters, setting, and problem by selecting pictures from sets of 3 that depict the element requested across 7 different stories, with 80% accuracy for each element, given indirect questions and expectant waiting.

Annual Goal: Student will demonstrate comprehension of story narratives by answering questions about main characters, settings, and problems across 10 different stories, with 80% accuracy for each element, independently.

CONTENT AREA: VOCABULARY DEVELOPMENT

Word Learning

Sample PLP for a five-year-old student with S/LI and cognitive impairment: Reportedly, student is minimally verbal (that is, at the 1–2 word response level), but has made a lot of progress this year in the area of comprehension. While student is beginning to understand some of the more experientially based words such as the verbs *go, stop, push, pull*, and the concepts *big* and *little,* his grasp of them is sketchy, at best. These difficulties impact his ability to follow directions and derive benefit from the kindergarten curriculum. They also interfere with peer relations.

Goal/Objective Templates Based on PLP

Short-Term Objective 1: Given demonstration and modeling in a play-based setting, student will demonstrate comprehension of 4 experientially based vocabulary words by performing the appropriate action on objects (for example, push the car) when asked, 8/10 opportunities, across different people and activities, given a combination of direct verbal and manual sign cues.

Short-Term Objective 2: Given multisensory experiences in a play-based setting, student will demonstrate comprehension of 3 additional vocabulary words and maintenance of the previous 4 by performing the appropriate action on objects when asked, 8/10 opportunities, across different people and activities, given a combination of indirect verbal and gestural cues.

Short-Term Objective 3: Given multisensory experiences in a play-based setting, student will demonstrate comprehension of 3 additional vocabulary words and maintenance of the previous 7 by performing the appropriate action on objects when asked, 9/10 opportunities, across different people and activities, given gestural cues.

Annual Goal: Student will demonstrate comprehension of 10 vocabulary words in play activities by performing the appropriate action on objects, 9/10 opportunities, across different people and activities, given expectant time delay.

Comprehending Wh-Questions

Sample PLP for a four-year-old with S/LI: Student scores below grade level on the *Peabody Picture Vocabulary Test (PPVT)* and the *Comprehensive Assessment of Spoken Language (CASL).* She has particular difficulty answering *who, what, when,* and *where* questions. This affects her ability to pay attention during story time and to demonstrate her understanding of story content.

Short-Term Objective 1: Given prior direct teaching and accompanying manual signs for Wh-questions, student will demonstrate comprehension of 10 each *where* and *who* questions, by responding appropriately to them across a minimum of 3 play-based activities, at a 70% accuracy level for each word category, given direct verbal cues.

Short-Term Objective 2:   Given manual signs for Wh-questions, student will demonstrate comprehension of 10 each *when* and *what* questions, and maintenance of 10 previously learned *where* and *who* questions, by responding appropriately to them across a minimum of 3 play-based activities and 3 stories, at an 80% accuracy level for each word category, given direct and indirect verbal cues.

Short-Term Objective 3:   Given manual signs for Wh-questions, student will demonstrate comprehension of 10 each *where, who, when,* and *what* questions, by responding appropriately to them across a minimum of 3 play-based activities and 3 stories, at a 90% accuracy level for each word category, given indirect verbal cues as needed.

Annual Goal: Given manual signs for Wh-questions, student will demonstrate comprehension of novel *where, who, when,* and *what* questions, by responding appropriately to them across stories and classroom activities at an accuracy level of 90% for each word category, independently.

Understanding Attributes

Sample PLP for a sixteen-year-old student with high-functioning autism: Although student has a large and relatively sophisticated vocabulary, she has difficulty comprehending directives in both her day-to-day academic activities and in her interactions with peers. Her speech-language pathologist (SLP) reports that in observing student during her participation in a game involving clues, student does not comprehend many of the attributes, as judged by her erroneous responses to the questions of peers. Student's comprehension difficulty affects her interactions with classmates; her ability to understand verbal directives; and her ability to process information in a timely fashion in her tenth-grade inclusive classroom setting.

Goal/Objective Templates Based on PLP

Short-Term Objective 1:   Given direct teaching and accompanying visual cues, student will demonstrate comprehension of 6 attributes/descriptors by responding appropriately to contextually relevant questions in therapist-designed activities, 8/10 opportunities, given direct verbal cues/correction.

Short-Term Objective 2:   Given accompanying visual cues, student will demonstrate comprehension of 4 new attributes/descriptors, and maintenance of the previous 6, by responding appropriately to contextually relevant questions in therapist-designed activities, 8/10 opportunities, given indirect verbal cues/ teacher correction.

Short-Term Objective 3: Given accompanying visual cues, student will demonstrate comprehension of 2 new attributes/descriptors, and maintenance of the previous 10, by responding appropriately to contextually relevant questions across a variety of classroom activities, 8/10 opportunities, given teacher correction, as needed.

Annual Goal: Student will demonstrate comprehension of 15 attributes/descriptors by responding appropriately to contextually relevant questions across classroom activities, 9/10 opportunities, given minimal need for teacher correction.

CONTENT AREA: NONVERBAL CUES AND SIGNALS

Comprehending Paralinguistic Features

Sample PLP for a thirteen-year-old student with NLD: Both informal observation in academic settings and formal language testing indicate that student's receptive and expressive vocabulary is within normal limits. This contrasts sharply with his ability to comprehend the nonverbal cues and signals that accompany verbal input, particularly as they relate to sarcasm and irony. His teachers report that student is often the object of ridicule and teasing because he takes what he hears literally and fails to take into account the tone of voice or body language that change the meaning of the words. This problem affects his relationship with peers, as well as his ability to understand the motivations of characters in stories.

Goal/Objective Templates Based on PLP

Short-Term Objective 1: Given direct instruction regarding nonverbal cues and 10 sample videotaped vignettes, student will demonstrate the ability to discriminate between literal and sarcastic utterances by identifying the correct characterization of each within a forced-choice format (true-meaning or sarcastic), with 80% accuracy, given direct verbal cues and teacher correction.

Short-Term Objective 2: Given 10 familiar sample videotaped vignettes, student will demonstrate his understanding of sarcasm by choosing the correct responses to the previously identified sarcastic utterances from groups of 3 possible options, with 80% accuracy, given indirect verbal cues and teacher correction, as needed.

Short-Term Objective 3: Given 10 novel role-play scenarios, student will demonstrate understanding of sarcastic utterances by responding appropriately to them, 80% of opportunities, given expectant waiting as needed.

Annual Goal: Student will demonstrate the ability to discriminate between literal and sarcastic utterances by responding to them appropriately across classroom settings with 80% accuracy, independently.

Explanatory Note: A great way to ensure an unending supply of videotaped role-plays individualized to the specific needs of students is to seek out volunteers from the school drama club to act out therapist- and teacher-written scripts.

Reading Body Language

Sample PLP for an eleven-year-old student with NLD: Student demonstrates strengths in those aspects of language that do not rely on nonverbal information (for example, dealing with facts). Although she is making progress in reading the facial expressions of others in her language therapy class, she evidences body language and facial expressions that many of her classmates find menacing. This difficulty has caused many of her peers to avoid her or call her cruel names.

Short-Term Objective 1:   Given direct instruction regarding specific aspects of body language/facial expressions and 5 videotaped role-play scenarios, student will state whether the behavior observed is engaging or off-putting, and select from a 3-card multiple choice format the reason for her answer, at an 80% level of accuracy, given indirect verbal cues.

Short-Term Objective 2:   Given 5 new videotaped role-plays, student will state whether the behavior observed is engaging or off-putting and state the reason for her answer, at an 80% level of accuracy, given manual sign cues.

Short-Term Objective 3:   Given 5 specific scenarios for role-play and a set of 3 possible body-language scripts for each (highly appropriate; acceptable; inappropriate), student will select 1 of 2 appropriate responses and act out the role-play with a peer, using appropriate body language/facial expressions 80% of the time, as judged according to a 5-point rating scale for determining appropriateness. (Role-plays will be videotaped and analyzed by the student, according to preset parameters, with indirect verbal cueing by SLP, as needed.)

Annual Goal: Given minimal indirect verbal cues, student will act out 5 role-play scenarios with a peer, using appropriate body language and facial expressions 80% of the time, as judged according to a 5-point rating scale for determining appropriateness, independently.

GENERAL TEACHING TIPS AND STRATEGIES FOR COMPREHENSION

1. Provide students with frequent, repetitive language input, delivered in short units of speech, and with accompanying manual signs/visual supports whenever possible to supplement the auditory channel.

2. Avoid *testing* students by constantly asking questions. Instead, *teach* them by providing the information they need to establish the connections that lead to meaning.

3. Organize the resource room curriculum (as well as tasks in inclusive settings) around concepts and vocabulary that are functional for the student (that is, that directly relate to the student's life experiences).

4. In working with themes, incorporate those that are conceptually based or functionally relevant (for example, for younger students: sticky/smooth theme, big/little theme, and so on; for older students: going to a restaurant, doing the laundry, and so on). Although there is greater leeway for doing this in a specialized setting, it is possible to incorporate such things in inclusive settings as well. For example, supplement a transportation theme with basic concept themes of *fast* and *slow*.

5. Conduct experiential, multisensory, hands-on lessons in the preschool classroom to facilitate comprehension of word-object, word-action, and object-action associations, and to promote comprehension beyond the level of the simple object label.

6. Make use of multiple-choice formats where appropriate, particularly in the initial stages of skill development, because they help to structure the student's responses, thereby enabling him or her to be more successful.

7. Employ techniques and strategies that facilitate the student's ability to process information and understand directives. These include

   - Securing the student's attention before giving a direction

   - Simplifying language processing by breaking down multistep directions

   - Adding visual information to the directions such as

     - Objects or object miniatures

     - Picture cues

- Natural gestures

- Sign language (manual signs)

- Reducing extraneous auditory and visual distractions to the extent possible

- Encouraging the student to use repair strategies (to ask for repetition or clarification), when needed

8. Directly teach the meaning of idiomatic expressions/figurative language and address the multiple meanings of words in contexts that promote understanding. Provide contrived opportunities for repetition and practice.

9. Directly teach students to understand the meaning of nonverbal cues and signals in both contrived and natural situations. Provide practice opportunities, in context, through the use of structured role-plays.

10. Use color-coding and visual supports to concretize and directly teach difficult-to-grasp narrative elements [for example, blue = setting; orange = main character(s)].

CHAPTER

12

THE MANY DIFFERENT FACES OF EXPRESSION

"It is the supreme art of the teacher to awaken joy in creative expression and knowledge."

—*Albert Einstein*

RATIONALE FOR INCLUDING SKILL CATEGORY

- Pragmatic development, which consists of the pragmatic functions of communication and conversational rules, is the primary area of communication deficit in students with ASD (Twachtman-Cullen, 2000a, 2000b, 1998), and it looms large for students with NLD (Tanguay, 2001) as well. Moreover, depending on the specific area of pragmatics affected, it has been our experience that students in each of the other disability categories addressed also manifest difficulty in this complex area of human functioning.

- Joint attention, which involves triadic or shared attention, is considered a gateway to symbolic communication (Twachtman-Cullen, 2008) and is specifically impaired in ASD (Sigman, Mundy, Sherman, and Ungerer, 1986).

- More able students with ASD may also have difficulty with the use of higher-order pragmatic functions (Gillberg and Ehlers, 1998; Twachtman-Cullen, 2000a, 2000b, 1998) such as use of repair strategies, negotiating, dealing with sarcasm and irony, and so on.

Difficulty in these nuanced areas of communication development may also be manifested by students with ADD/ADHD, S/LI, NLD, and ED, although the reason for such difficulty may be more extrinsic than intrinsic.

- Difficulties are also seen in an additional area of pragmatics known as *presuppositional knowledge* (Twachtman-Cullen, 2000a, 2000b, 2000c) in students with ASD, and are also evidenced in students with NLD, given the nature of their impairment (Tanguay, 2001).

- Children with S/LI clearly have difficulties with various aspects of language expression.

- Narrative discourse skills are often negatively impacted in students with ASD, as a result of the documented deficits in critical thinking (Minshew, Goldstein, Taylor, and Siegel, 1994) and pragmatics (Twachtman-Cullen, 2000b, 2000c).

- Children with ADD/ADHD are more likely to have expressive as opposed to receptive language impairments, owing to their impulsive learning style and difficulties in inhibiting verbal responses.

PRESENT LEVELS OF PERFORMANCE FOR COMMUNICATION, EXPRESSION, AND NARRATIVE SKILLS

These should include

- A statement indicating the student's strengths in specific areas of communication, expression, or narrative skills, particularly as they relate to academic achievement and functional performance

- A statement about the student's weaknesses in specific areas of communication, expression, or narrative skills, particularly as they relate to academic achievement, functional performance, and priority educational needs for the coming year

Note that if the student is nonverbal or minimally verbal, it is important to include a statement about the student's current means of communication.

- A statement on how the student's disability in communication, expression, or narrative functioning, impacts his or her involvement and progress in the general curriculum (or, for preschool children, in appropriate activities)

- The sources of the statements in the PLP (optional)

- Any additional information that can enable the PLP to fulfill its two important functions: (1) to serve as the basis for generating need-based, individualized IEP goals and objectives; and (2) to serve as the standard by which to judge student performance and progress

CONTENT AREA: JOINT ATTENTION

Sample PLP for a five-year-old student with moderate ASD: Student will engage with his parents, teacher, and speech-language pathologist regarding items that he wants; however, he does not consistently respond to adults' attempts to direct his attention to interesting objects and events, even if they would likely be of interest to him. These difficulties prevent student from benefiting from the rich array of educational experiences in his kindergarten classroom.

Goal/Objective Templates Based on PLP

Short-Term Objective 1: Given the out-of-reach placement of a preferred item, student will respond to the directive "Look" plus communicative point by looking at the item and shifting his gaze back to the adult, 6/10 contrived opportunities in the therapy room or small group setting, given 1 or 2 repetitions of the direction, and a prompt to promote appropriate gaze shifting (for example, clearing one's throat to attract the child's attention).

Short-Term Objective 2: Given the out-of-reach placement of a preferred item, student will respond to the directive "Look" plus communicative point by looking at the item and shifting his gaze back to the adult, 8/10 contrived opportunities in the therapy room or small group setting, given a maximum of 1 repetition of the direction and a prompt to promote appropriate gaze shifting.

   Note that gaze shifting should be reinforced, immediately, in the two preceding objectives by obtaining the object for the child and allowing him to play with it for a few minutes.

Short-Term Objective 3: Given the out-of-reach placement of a preferred item, student will respond to the adult's communicative point by looking at the item and shifting his gaze back to the adult, independently, 8/10 contrived opportunities in the therapy room or small-group setting, given a prompt to promote appropriate gaze shifting, verbal praise, and the object.

Annual Goal: Student will respond to adults' joint-attention bids by looking at the object to which he has been directed, either verbally or gesturally, and then shifting his gaze back to the adult, 8/10 opportunities in the classroom, independently or with expectant waiting, as needed.

CONTENT AREA: PRAGMATIC FUNCTIONS OF COMMUNICATION

Requesting/Protesting (or Refusing/Rejecting)

Sample PLP for a four-year-old nonverbal student with severe autism: Student's teacher and speech-language pathologist report that she is quite self-sufficient—when she wants something, she will try to obtain it on her own. For example, if something is on a high shelf, student will usually bring a chair over to the area and attempt to climb on it to obtain what she desires. If a chair is unavailable, she will sometimes lead the adult to the object. Although student is able to give a photograph in an exchange format to request something, given cues, she does not appear to look at the photograph or connect it to the item she receives. Student's primitive, nonverbal communication skills often cause her a good deal of frustration. In addition, they not only prevent her from participating effectively in her special education classroom but also limit her mainstream experiences.

Goal/Objective Templates Based on PLP (Set One: Simple Requesting)

Short-Term Objective 1: Given the presence of preferred food and beverage items and the question (accompanied by manual signs), "What do you want?" student will request one or the other item by picking up the small representational object associated with it and placing it in the adult's open palm, 8/10 opportunities, across different food and beverage choices, and across different people, given hand-over-hand physical assistance by a third party (for example, paraprofessional).

Short-Term Objective 2: Given the presence of preferred food and beverage items and the question (accompanied by manual signs), "What do you want?" student will request one or the other item by picking up the small representational object associated with it and handing it to the adult, with an appropriate gaze shift to adult, 8/10 opportunities, across different food and beverage choices, and across different people, given minimal physical assistance (tapping the hand).

It should be noted that the gaze shift may be stimulated by holding the object at eye level. Or the adult could make a sound, such as clearing his or her throat, to attract the child's attention, and wait until she shifts her gaze to fulfill the request.

Short-Term Objective 3: Given the presence of preferred food and beverage items, and the indirect cue, "I have crackers and juice," student will request item(s) desired by selecting one or more small objects from an array of 2–3 different food, and 2–3 different beverage choices, and handing it (or them) to the adult, using an appropriate gaze shift, 8/10 opportunities, across different food and beverage choices, and across different people, given minimal gestural cues, as needed.

Explanatory Notes:

- The short-term objectives lend themselves to the following prompt fade-back plan: Adult asking "What do you want?" with hand extended to receive small object cue; proceeding to a direct verbal cue (for example, "What do you want?") without palm extended; then to an indirect verbal cue ("I have cheese and crackers," or "I have crackers and juice"); and then proceeding to gestural cue alone, expectant waiting, and finally to independent/initiated.

- To ensure that requesting is fully functional for the student in the snack routine, the generalization protocol should include different food and beverage choices, and the routine should be carried out by different people (for example, speech-language pathologist, teacher, paraprofessionals, and so on).

- Because the above stated PLP clearly indicates that the child was not attending to the pictures, the first short-term objective specified a more concrete requesting mode in the form of small representational objects. Eventually, objects should be paired with pictures to help the student to move toward greater abstraction.

Annual Goal: When presented with a snack tray, student will initiate requests for food and beverage items by selecting 1 or more small objects from an array of 3–5 and handing it (or them) to the adult while shifting gaze appropriately, 9/10 opportunities, across communication partners and a variety of food and beverage items. (There are no prompt levels specified, as student is required to initiate her request.)

Explanatory Note: Because individuals with autism evidence a situation-specific learning style, it should not be assumed that learning to request items in one venue will translate to being able to request different types of items in another. Hence, additional short-term objectives should be written in service to annual goals targeting *requesting toys, requesting activities,* or *requesting a break,* and the like.

Goal/Objective Templates Based on PLP (Set Two: Requesting/Rejecting Combined)

Short-Term Objective 1:   Given the presence of preferred and nonpreferred food and beverage items, student will refuse the nonpreferred item offered (via head shake, signing "no," gentle push-away gesture, and the like) and when asked, "What do you want?" will request 1 or the other item desired by handing the appropriate picture to the adult, 8/10 opportunities, across different food and beverage choices, and across different people, given direct verbal cues.

Short-Term Objective 2:   Given the presence of several preferred and nonpreferred food and beverage items, student will refuse 2 nonpreferred items offered and when asked, "What do you want?" will request 1 or 2 preferred items by handing the appropriate pictures to the adult 8/10 opportunities, across different food and beverage choices, and across different people, given indirect verbal cues.

Short-Term Objective 3:   Given the presence of preferred and nonpreferred toys or activities, student will refuse 2 nonpreferred toys or activities offered and when asked, "What do you want?" will request a preferred toy or activity by handing the appropriate picture to the adult 8/10 opportunities, across different toy/activity choices, and across different people, given expectant waiting or indirect verbal cues as needed.

Annual Goal: Student will appropriately refuse nonpreferred items and activities when offered, and will independently request those that are desired by handing an appropriate picture to an adult or peer, across a variety of classroom activities.

Sample PLP for an eight-year-old student with ADHD and S/LI: According to teacher and parent report, although student is able to use a variety of appropriate means to protest/refuse items and activities, due to his impulsivity he only does so in calm, highly structured situations when prompted to do so. Most of the time, he protests or requests termination of activities through the use of undesirable behavior, such as throwing objects or dropping to the floor. His behavior affects his ability to engage in activities with peers in both classroom and extracurricular settings without extensive supervision by staff, and worsens in less-structured settings.

Goal/Objective Templates Based on PLP (Set One: Refusing)

Short-Term Objective 1:   When offered nonpreferred items or activities in a calm, preferred setting, student will reject undesired objects or activities by saying "no," 7/10 opportunities, across different items or activities and people, given manual-sign/gestural cues, as needed.

Short-Term Objective 2:   When offered nonpreferred items or activities in a calm, preferred setting, student will reject undesired objects or activities by saying "no," 8/10 opportunities, across different items or activities and people, given expectant waiting.

Short-Term Objective 3:   When offered nonpreferred items or activities in contrived situations in a variety of nonstructured, noisy settings (for example, lunch, recess, physical education), student will reject undesired items or activities by saying "no," 7/10 opportunities, with manual sign cue to *wait* before responding.

Annual Goal: When offered a choice of objects or activities, student will reject those that are undesired by saying "no," independently, 8/10 opportunities across settings and people, with minimal gestural cues as needed.

Goal/Objective Templates Based on PLP (Set Two: Terminating an Activity)

Short Term Objective 1:   Given a STOP card, directions regarding its use, and a calm, structured setting, student will request termination of a nonpreferred activity by saying "stop" or handing the card to the adult, 7/10 opportunities, across a variety of activities and people, given direct verbal and manual-sign cues for *stop*.

Short-Term Objective 2:   Given a nonstructured setting (recess or physical education) and informed participants, student will request termination of a semipreferred activity by saying or signing "stop," 7/10 opportunities, across a variety of activities and people, given direct or indirect verbal cues.

Short-Term Objective 3:   Given a nonstructured setting (recess or physical education) and informed participants, student will request termination of a nonpreferred activity by saying or signing "stop," 8/10 opportunities, across a variety of activities and people, given minimal indirect gestural cueing/expectant waiting (for example, palms up to indicate *What are you supposed to do?*).

Annual Goal: Student will appropriately request termination of an activity across settings and people, independently, 9/10 opportunities.

Obtaining Attention

Sample PLP for a fourteen-year-old moderately verbal student with ASD: According to clinical observation and teacher report, student is able to effectively communicate her desires during a classroom snack routine when staff is attending to her, or when they specifically ask her what she wants. When staff is not attending to her, however, she will just sit and wait for a prompt. Both her speech-language pathologist and teacher are concerned that she is becoming increasingly prompt-dependent. These difficulties impact student's ability to independently get her needs met in both her special education classroom and in the mainstream settings to which she is assigned.

Goal/Objective Templates Based on PLP

Short-Term Objective 1:   Given direct teaching, demonstration, and modeling, student will obtain the attention of an adult prior to making a request by tapping the adult's arm or saying his or her name during a proximate activity (for example, snack routine or game), 7/10 opportunities, across different activities and people, given physical assistance and direct verbal cues.

Short-Term Objective 2:   Given planned inattention and waiting, student will obtain the attention of an adult prior to making a request by tapping the adult's arm or saying his or her name during a proximate activity (for example, snack routine or game), 8/10 opportunities, across different activities and people, given indirect verbal or gestural cues.

Short-Term Objective 3:   Given planned inattention and waiting by an informed adult, student will obtain the attention of the adult prior to making a request by raising her hand, 8/10 opportunities, across different activities and people, given manual sign cue to *wait* as needed.

Annual Goal: Student will obtain the adult's attention prior to making a request by raising her hand and waiting for the adult to respond, independently, 8/10 opportunities, across settings, activities, and people.

Explanatory Notes:

- The reference to "planned inattention" above is meant to underscore that if a student is being taught to request attention, he or she should not already have the adult's attention! Although it should go without saying, in our experience it rarely does.

- A third-party "coach" should be used to prompt attention to the target adult, so that the student can legitimately obtain his or her attention.

Informing/Clarifying

Sample PLP for a ten-year-old student with ADD: Student evidences an impulsive learning style in which she quickly blurts out answers to verbal questions and fails to think through answers on quizzes and tests. She becomes particularly confused when she is required to make judgments about things that, though largely similar, differ in important ways. Her failure to take attributes into account causes her to make careless errors in her written work, tests, and class discussions. As a result, student's grades in several academic subjects have been negatively affected.

Goal/Objective Templates Based on PLP

Short-Term Objective 1: Given direct instruction in a referential communication task (barrier game), an array of 10 small stationary objects (for example, 2 "dollhouse" tables, 2 beds, 2 chairs, 2 sinks, and 2 baskets) that differ only in one dimension (for example, size or color), and the directive to listen, student will ask the question, "Which table (chair, and so on)?" (answer: the *big* one or the *red* one) when directed to place 10 moveable objects (for example, shoe, doll, apple, and so on) *in, on,* and *under* each of the stationary items, 6/10 opportunities, given manual *wait* sign, direct verbal cue, and teacher correction or praise.

Explanatory Note: The information in parentheses above is offered only for clarification purposes here. It may be omitted in actual short-term objectives.

Short-Term Objective 2: Given a barrier game, an array of 10 small stationary objects that differ only in one dimension (for example, size or color), and the directive paired with the manual sign to listen, student will ask the question, "Which [object name]?" when directed to place 10 moveable objects *in, on,* and *under* each of the stationary items, 9/10 opportunities, given manual *wait* sign and indirect verbal cue ("What did you forget?"), and teacher correction or praise.

Short-Term Objective 3: Given a barrier game, the manual sign for *listen,* and an array of 12 small stationary objects that differ in two dimensions (for example, size *and* color), student will ask the question, "Which [object name?]" when directed to place 12 moveable objects *in, on,* and *under* each of the stationary items, 9/10 opportunities, given teacher correction or praise. (For example, in answer to the question, "which chair" the adult responds "the *big* chair." However, there are 2 big chairs that differ only in color, requiring the child to ask, "Which *big* chair?" Answer: the *red* chair.)

Annual Goal: Given directives involving items that are similar along different dimensions (for example, red pen/blue pen), student will ask the appropriate question to obtain the information that she needs, 9/10 opportunities, across classroom activities, independently.

Negotiating

Sample PLP for a fifteen-year-old student with ED: Student is able to complete academic work with regular breaks; however, he often becomes angry when he needs to put away preferred items in order to return to an academic task. He also has difficulty negotiating with peers in social situations. This difficulty causes considerable disruption in his high school classes; impairs his social relationships; and compromises both the quantity and quality of academic work that he is able to complete.

Goal/Objective Templates Based on PLP

Short-Term Objective 1: Given direct instruction in negotiation techniques, and 5 structured "flexible" scenarios that lend themselves to further modifications, student will select the appropriate negotiation strategy (for example, "Please"; "Just a little longer"; "Can I do just one?" and so on) from a group of 3 options presented, 4/5 opportunities, across different people, given direct and indirect verbal cues.

Short-Term Objective 2: Given 5 structured "flexible" scenarios that lend themselves to further modifications, student will apply the appropriate negotiation strategy in a variety of structured role-play situations with 1 peer and 1 adult, 4/5 opportunities, given indirect verbal cues.

Short-Term Objective 3: Given 7 structured "flexible" scenarios that lend themselves to further modifications, student will apply the appropriate negotiation strategy in structured role-play situations with a peer, 6/7 opportunities, given minimal cues, as needed.

Annual Goal: Given a group project containing several opportunities for negotiation, student will apply the appropriate negotiation strategy in the classroom setting, 80% of opportunities, given indirect verbal cues, as needed.

CONTENT AREA: REPAIRING COMMUNICATION BREAKDOWNS

Obtaining Clarification

Sample PLP for a twelve-year-old student with ASD: Student's speech-language pathologist reports that he communicates for a variety of purposes including *obtaining attention, requesting, protesting,* and *commenting.* In fact, he appears to have mastered most of the lower-level pragmatic functions of communication. He experiences difficulty, however, with higher-order functions such as the use of repair strategies (for example, asking for clarification if he doesn't understand something). These difficulties impact student's ability to function in his seventh-grade inclusive classroom setting and in extracurricular activities as well.

Goal/Objective Templates Based on PLP

Short-Term Objective 1: Given direct instruction and a variety of situations in which verbal clarification is needed, student will select the appropriate repair-strategy card from a group of three to obtain clarification (repair strategies to include: "Please repeat that"; "What do you mean?"; "I need more information") to inform the listener of the need for clarification, 4/5 opportunities within a variety of structured role-plays, across different people, given manual sign and direct verbal cues as needed

Short-Term Objective 2: Given a variety of situations in which verbal clarification is needed, student will use repair strategies appropriate to each situation to inform the listener of the need for clarification, 4/5 opportunities in a variety of structured role-plays, across different people, given manual sign and indirect verbal cues as needed.

Short-Term Objective 3: Given contrived situations in which verbal clarification is needed, student will use appropriate repair strategies to inform the listener of the need for clarification, 4/5 opportunities in the classroom setting, given gestural cues as needed.

Annual Goal: Given the need for verbal clarification, student will use appropriate repair strategies in contrived situations to inform the listener of the need for clarification, 4/5 opportunities across academic settings, given expectant waiting and minimal indirect verbal reminders.

Sample PLP for a nine-year-old student with S/LI: Student is able to answer direct questions, but often does not ask questions to obtain information that she needs to carry out assignments. As a result, she frequently misunderstands assignments because she is missing important information. These difficulties negatively impact school performance in her third-grade classroom, and interfere with her ability to complete homework assignments.

Goal/Objective Templates Based on PLP

Short-Term Objective 1:   Given examples, modeling, and a series of props, student will ask questions using Wh- and other question forms in order to obtain needed information in contextually appropriate situations and activities, 8/10 opportunities within a variety of structured role-plays, across different people, given manual sign (for *where* or *what*) to cue the question. (For example, the adult directs student to "Put the paper in the folder." Because student has 3 folders—that is, props—in front of her, she needs to ask, "Which folder?")

Short-Term Objective 2:   Given a series of props, student will ask questions using Wh- and other question forms in order to obtain needed information in contextually appropriate situations and activities, 8/10 opportunities within a variety of structured role-plays, across different people, given expectant waiting.

Short-Term Objective 3:   Given contrived "real-world" situations, student will ask questions using Wh- and other question forms in order to obtain needed information in the classroom setting, 8/10 opportunities, with minimal indirect verbal cues.

Annual Goal: Student will ask questions using Wh- and other question forms in order to obtain needed information in contextually appropriate situations and activities, 8/10 opportunities, across academic subjects, given expectant waiting.

Explanatory Note: The use of the phrase *contrived "real-world" situations* refers to the deliberate structuring of tasks in natural settings. For example, to facilitate generalization to the classroom setting, the adult should deliberately withhold important information or give ambiguous directions for the purpose of creating a need for the student to ask for additional information.

CONTENT AREA: CONVERSATIONAL RULES

Reciprocity

Sample PLP for a five-year-old student with ASD and S/LI: Student desires to interact with others but often withdraws because she appears not to know what to say next. She is particularly lacking in the typical social phrases that are used by young children in their play activities. When her teacher tells her what to say, she will repeat it, but often does not use the word or phrase in the next interaction where it is appropriate to do so. This difficulty negatively impacts her ability to participate in classroom activities and to participate effectively in childhood games with peers.

Goal/Objective Templates Based on PLP

Short-Term Objective 1: Given direct instruction in 3 common social phrases (for example, "I got it"; "Your turn," and so on), and accompanying manual sign cues, student will apply these phrases in contextually appropriate activities in role-play situations with 1 peer, 4/5 opportunities, given direct verbal and manual sign cues to use phrases.

Short-Term Objective 2: Given direct instruction in 2 new common social phrases and maintenance of the previously learned 3, each of which are accompanied by manual sign cues, student will apply these phrases in contextually appropriate activities in role-play situations with 1 peer, 4/5 opportunities, given expectant waiting.

Short-Term Objective 3: Given a game format, student will apply appropriate social phrases from the 5 previously learned within the context of a familiar game with 2 peers, 4/5 opportunities, given expectant waiting.

Annual Goal: Student will apply social phrases in contextually appropriate activities in the classroom during interactions with peers, 4/5 opportunities, independently or with expectant waiting.

Sample PLP for a fourteen-year-old student with NLD: By teacher and parent report, student appears to enjoy interacting with others. She will frequently approach adults and peers to greet them. After the greeting, however, she appears unsure of how to keep the conversation going. She has the most difficulty with small talk, which significantly impacts her ability to interact socially with peers in extracurricular activities.

Goal/Objective Templates Based on PLP

Short-Term Objective 1: Given direct instruction, demonstration, and a series of scenarios, student will select the appropriate "conversation fillers" from 6 options presented, to fill her turn in conversations with at least 1 informed adult in structured role-play situations, for a minimum of 3 turns, given direct verbal cues as needed.

Short-Term Objective 2:   Given a series of scenarios, student will select appropriate "conversation fillers" from 8 options presented, to fill her turn in conversations with an uninformed adult in structured role-play situations, for a minimum of 4 turns given minimal indirect verbal or gestural cues.

Short-Term Objective 3:   Given manual signs to prompt "conversation filler," student will fill her turn in conversations with 1 informed peer in structured role-play situations, for 4 turns, given expectant waiting, as needed.

Annual Goal: Student will fill her turn in conversations with 1 adult or peer within the classroom setting, for a minimum of 3–4 turns, with minimal indirect cueing.

Staying on Topic

Sample PLP for a nine-year-old student with ASD: Student is a very verbal child who enjoys discussing topics of interest with others, according to clinical observation and teacher report; however, student has problems carrying on conversations with others when he does not choose the topic. Under these conditions, he has great difficulty staying on topic, as evidenced by his tendency to change the subject (usually to one that centers on his interests) or make tangential comments. This difficulty impacts his ability to communicate effectively with both adults and peers, and is especially off-putting to the latter. Overall, student's difficulties negatively impact his ability to establish relationships with peers, and set him apart from classmates in his inclusive classroom setting.

Goal/Objective Templates Based on PLP

Short-Term Objective 1:   Given direct instruction in what it means to stay on topic, and a series of discussion topics containing elements that he finds moderately interesting, student will demonstrate the ability to select conversational sentence strips from a group of 3 options that are appropriate to the topics, across 5 topics for 3 turns, 8/10 opportunities, across people, given direct verbal cues paired with manual sign cues.

Short-Term Objective 2:   Given a series of discussion topics containing elements that he finds moderately interesting, student will demonstrate the ability to select conversational sentence strips from a group of 3 options that are appropriate to the topics, across 5 previous and 5 new topics for 4 turns, 8/10 opportunities, across people, given indirect verbal cues.

Short-Term Objective 3:   Given a series of discussion topics that he finds minimally interesting, student will demonstrate the ability to stay on topic by filling his conversational turn with statements/questions that are appropriate to the topic under discussion, across 5 new topics for 3 turns in structured role-plays with adults and peers, 4/5 opportunities, given indirect verbal cues.

Annual Goal: Given discussion topics that he finds minimally interesting, student will demonstrate the ability to stay on topic by filling his conversational turn with statements/questions that are appropriate to the topic under discussion, across topics for a minimum of 4 turns in structured role-plays with adults and peers, 4/5 opportunities, independently.

Presuppositional Knowledge

This type of knowledge enables people to adjust what they say (content), as well as the manner in which they express it (style), to the contours of the social situation. For example, one would use a soft voice and speak differently in a hospital intensive care unit than at a baseball game. Similarly, one would adjust the content and manner of expression when speaking to a person in authority rather than with a close friend. The ability to make appropriate presuppositions regarding situational requirements to inform language content is a significant area of deficit in students with ASD and NLD; however, given the impulsivity associated with ADD/ADHD, and the self-focus that is seen in many students with ED, it is our opinion that this area of social cognition is a critically important one in these disability categories as well.

Sample PLP for an eighteen-year-old student with NLD: According to formal testing, observations of her teachers, and parent report, student has an excellent command of vocabulary, grammar, and syntax. She is doing very well in her academic setting where adults and peers who know her well accept her social idiosyncrasies. Problems arise, however, in her school-related work-study program. Reportedly, she has made inappropriate personal comments to both her supervisor and customers. Student's lack of appreciation for the situational requirements of the work setting place her at-risk for losing her job.

Goal/Objective Templates Based on PLP

Short-Term Objective 1:   Given direct instruction regarding "business" versus "personal" talk, demonstration/modeling of appropriate and inappropriate comments, and a series of work-related scenarios, student will select from a multiple-choice format comments appropriate to the scenario, for 7/10 opportunities, given indirect verbal cueing and correction.

Short-Term Objective 2:   Given a series of work-related scenarios, student will select from multiple-choice format comments appropriate to the scenario, for 8/10 opportunities, independently.

Short-Term Objective 3:   Given a series of work-related scenarios and a list containing "business-related" and "personal" comments, student will apply appropriate comments in structured role-plays with an adult, 8/10 opportunities, given indirect verbal cues or expectant waiting as needed.

Annual Goal: Given contrived situations based on those previously addressed, student will apply appropriate comments, across conversations with adults in her work-study setting, 4/5 opportunities, given minimal, indirect verbal cueing and correction, as needed.

Sentence Formulation

Sample PLP for an eight-year-old student with S/LI: Student is a verbal child who will often initiate interactions with others. Formal testing and informal assessment indicate, however, that student has significant difficulties with sentence formulation. Specifically, when asked a question, student will often pantomime his response. When cued to use words, he will either give a one-word response, or say that he doesn't know the answer. When student initiates language, his speech is characterized by multiple grammatical errors and difficulty with word order. These problems affect his ability to participate effectively in the classroom curriculum, and adversely affect his grades and relationships with peers.

Goal/Objective Templates Based on PLP

Short-Term Objective 1:   Given a color-coded visual template for *subject, verb,* and *object,* and direct instruction in its use, student will answer questions by producing sentences of 3–5 words in length, in the correct order, for 7/10 questions given direct verbal and manual sign cues vis-à-vis use of the template.

Short-Term Objective 2:   Given a color-coded visual template for *subject, verb*, and *object,* student will answer questions by producing sentences of 5–7 words in length, in the correct order, for 8/10 different questions, given indirect verbal or gestural cues vis-à-vis use of the template.

Short-Term Objective 3:   Given a color-coded visual template for *subject, verb,* and *object,* student will answer questions by producing sentences from 7–10 words in length, in the correct order, for 8/10 different questions, given minimal gestural cues or expectant waiting.

Annual Goal: Given a visual color-coded template for *subject, verb,* and *object,* student will answer questions by producing sentences of 7 or more words in the correct order, within structured language arts activities in the classroom for 8/10 opportunities, given gestural cueing to use template as needed.

CONTENT AREA: NARRATIVE DEVELOPMENT

Generating Written Narratives

Sample PLP for an eleven-year-old student with NLD and ED: While student presents with strengths in verbal skills, his narrative skills cluster at the four- to five-year-old level, according to informal assessment tasks. His narratives are characterized by disorganized heaps of information rather than a sequentially organized series of events. These difficulties strongly impact student's ability to generate written narratives across academic subjects in his inclusive classroom setting, and generally interfere with his ability to demonstrate what he knows on quizzes and tests.

Goal/Objective Templates Based on PLP

Short-Term Objective 1:   Given a color-coded story format with accompanying pictures, and instruction in its use, student will generate a complete, written narrative containing the elements of *character, setting, time, problem event,* and *solution* across 3/5 stories, given direct and indirect verbal cues.

Short-Term Objective 2:   Given a color-coded story format with accompanying pictures, student will generate a complete, written narrative containing the elements of *character, setting, time, problem event,* and *solution* across 4/5 different stories, given indirect verbal cues.

Short-Term Objective 3:   Given a color-coded story format with accompanying pictures, student will generate a complete, written narrative containing the elements of *character, setting, time, problem event,* and *solution* across 9/10 different stories, independently.

Annual Goal: Given a color-coded story format with the words *character, setting, time, problem event,* and *solution* written on the segments, student will generate written book reports containing those elements in the classroom setting, independently.

Explanatory Note: Independent performance is still contingent upon the underlying condition: *the use of a color-coded story format.* Use of this formatting tool is considered an accommodation to enable successful student performance.

Narrative Discourse

Sample PLP for a seven-year-old student with ADHD: Student presents with excellent decoding skills that place her at grade level in this area. When assessed using a multiple-choice format, she even appears to be able to comprehend "straightforward" (that is, factual) information reasonably well. Problems occur, however, when she is asked to retell a story, or a past event. Under these circumstances, student is "all over the board"—that is, she mentions things out of sequence or fails to mention them at all. This difficulty impedes student's ability to participate in language arts and reading activities in her second-grade classroom, as well as in other activities involving narrative discourse.

Goal/Objective Templates Based on PLP

Short-Term Objective 1:   Given direct instruction in using a time line template for sequencing, and visual supports corresponding to a recent past event (for example, photographs of a field trip or other event), student will place the pictures in the appropriate sequence as she retells the event, incorporating the following elements: *participants, setting, time,* and at least 1 *activity,* across 5 events, 4/5 opportunities for all elements, given direct verbal and manual sign cues.

Short-Term Objective 2:   Given a time line template and visual supports corresponding to a recent past event, student will retell the event, incorporating the following elements: *participants, setting, time,* and at least 2 *activities*, across 5 new and 5 previous events, 4/5 opportunities for all elements, given indirect verbal or gestural cues.

Short-Term Objective 3:   Given a time line template and a checklist of story elements (*character, setting, time,* and *activities*), student will reformulate a story that has just been read to her, by placing pictures that incorporate the story elements on the template in the appropriate sequence, and then retelling the story across 5 different stories, 4/5 opportunities, given indirect verbal cues.

Annual Goal: Given a time line template and a checklist of story elements, student will verbally retell a story or event in the appropriate time sequence, incorporating the elements of *character, setting, time,* and *activities* across 10 different stories or events in the language arts curriculum, 8/10 opportunities, with minimal gestural cueing to use template/checklist.

GENERAL TEACHING TIPS AND STRATEGIES FOR COMMUNICATION, EXPRESSION, AND NARRATIVE DEVELOPMENT

1. Set up or structure situations to encourage communication. Some examples:

   - Snack time (wait for the student to request; give small portions; wait for the student to obtain your attention, and so on)

   - Place needed/desired items out of reach (for example, glue, crayons, a favorite toy, and so on) so that the student has a reason to communicate.

   - Offer the student things that you know he or she doesn't like in order to elicit an appropriate refusal (pragmatic protest function).

   - Skip a desired part of a well-known routine, so that the student has a reason and opportunity to supply needed information, or to request continuance.

   - Model commenting behavior and provide activities that are interesting and motivating to the student to facilitate spontaneous comments.

   - Increase salience wherever and whenever possible (for example, use color to highlight information, make things "larger than life").

   - Bring in a motivating toy, pet, or interesting object to provide both an impetus and context for communication and expression.

   - "Misunderstand" or "play dumb" to create a need for the student to provide expanded input.

   - Follow the student's lead in terms of his or her interests.

2. Use referential communication tasks (that is, barrier games) to demonstrate and teach the power of communication in a motivating context.

These can be designed by speech-language pathologists and are excellent vehicles for use in speech-language therapy and social, play, and leisure activities with peers.

3. Use demonstration and modeling of target responses (for example, nonverbal behavior, words, and phrases) whenever possible so that the student has a model of the appropriate behavior.

4. Use visual supports such as manual signs and sentence strips to facilitate the use of longer, more sophisticated utterances.

5. Give the student access to a variety of means of communication that he or she can use to initiate interactions, and be sure to reinforce by responding!

6. Use manual signs to help facilitate both word retrieval and sentence expansion.

7. Provide students with multimodal language input and feedback, including, but not limited to, the use of natural gestures, manual signs, pictures, written words, and so on, because they help facilitate comprehension and processing, which form the basis for meaningful expression.

CHAPTER

13

ALL THINGS SOCIAL

"Piglet sidled up to Pooh from behind. 'Pooh!' he whispered. 'Yes, Piglet?' 'Nothing,' said Piglet, taking Pooh's paw. 'I just wanted to be sure of you.'"

—*A. A. Milne*

RATIONALE FOR INCLUDING SKILL CATEGORY

- Research demonstrates that children with autism present with deficits in the development of imagination (Peeters and Gillberg, 1999; Twachtman-Cullen, 2000a) and symbolic play (Wolfberg, 2009). Tanguay (2001) also lists play as an area in need of remediation in NLD.

- Students with ADD/ADHD often have significant difficulties with peer relationships, owing to their impulsivity and self-regulation issues (Rief, 2005). In addition, given the nature of the anger-management issues and thought disturbances that characterize many students with ED, they too have difficulty establishing and maintaining social relationships. These issues also negatively impact play behavior in young children.

- Students with NLD fail to integrate verbal and nonverbal information or to innately understand that behavior appropriate for one audience may not be appropriate for another (Tanguay, 2001).

- Impairment in social behavior is a well-recognized hallmark feature of ASD, affecting social understanding and expression; social relatedness; and social interaction. According to Tanguay (2001), children with NLD have many of the same types of social cognitive problems as do children on the autism spectrum.

- Research demonstrates that individuals with ASD present with wide-ranging deficits in a type of social cognition known as *theory of mind* (Baron-Cohen, Tager-Flusberg, and Cohen, 1993; Hobson, 1989; Tager-Flusberg and Sullivan, 1994). Deficits in this domain make it difficult for the student to use external behavior—much of which is nonverbal—to predict internal states of mind, and thus make sense of behavior. Problems in theory of mind also make it difficult for students to take the perspective of another and to empathize.

- Students with NLD have very similar deficits in theory of mind to those with ASD, given their profound difficulty in reading nonverbal cues and signals, and failing to integrate verbal with nonverbal cues (Tanguay, 2001). Likewise, students with ADD/ADHD and those with ED also exhibit problems with perspective taking and empathy that likely reflect weak theory of mind skills.

PRESENT LEVELS OF PERFORMANCE FOR SOCIAL COGNITION, PLAY, AND LEISURE SKILL DEVELOPMENT

This should include

- A statement indicating the student's strengths in areas of social cognition, play (for young children), or leisure skill development, particularly as they relate to academic achievement (if appropriate) and functional performance

- If addressing play, it would be helpful to include the child's level of play skills development (solitary, parallel, associative, and so on)

- A statement about the student's weaknesses in specific areas of social cognition, play (for young children), or leisure skill development, particularly as they relate to academic achievement (if appropriate), functional performance, and priority educational needs for the coming year

- A statement on how the student's disability in the areas of social cognition, play (for young children), or leisure skill development impacts his or her involvement and progress in the general curriculum (or, for preschool children, in appropriate activities)

- The sources of the statements in the PLP (optional)

- Any additional information that can enable the PLP to fulfill its two important functions: (1) to serve as the basis for generating need-based, individualized IEP goals and objectives; and (2) to serve as the standard by which to judge student performance and progress

CONTENT AREA: SOCIAL COGNITION

Social Responding/Social Reciprocity

Sample PLP for a three-year-old student with severe autism and cognitive impairment: According to informal assessment and parent report, student presents with social-pragmatic skills that cluster in the 3–6 month range. He is most attentive to musical and rhythmic activities, and is beginning to enjoy mirror play. However, student demonstrates severe difficulties in responding to others and in social reciprocity (the back-and-forth social exchange that is the foundation for two-way conversational interactions). These difficulties affect his ability to participate in activities in his preschool program, particularly those involving social interactions.

Goal/Objective Templates Based on PLP

Short-Term Objective 1: Given a developmentally appropriate, motivating activity, delivered at a slow, nonthreatening pace, student will demonstrate appropriate social responding through eye contact or positive affect in 2 social games (for example, peek-a-boo; pat-a-cake) with an adult, for 4 turns, for 7/10 opportunities, given verbal praise.

Short-Term Objective 2: Given developmentally appropriate, motivating activities, delivered at a slow, nonthreatening pace, student will demonstrate appropriate social responding through eye contact or positive affect in 4 social activities (for example, the previous 2 social games and the songs *Row Row Row Your Boat* and *London Bridge Is Falling Down*) with an adult, for 5–7 turns, for 8/10 opportunities, given verbal praise.

Short-Term Objective 3: Given developmentally appropriate, motivating activities (delivered at an appropriate pace), student will demonstrate both appropriate social responding through eye contact or positive affect and social reciprocity through gestures (for example, attempting to clap in pat-a-cake; use blanket in peek-a-boo, and so on) in 4 social games/songs with an adult for 4–6 turns, for 8/10 opportunities, given verbal praise.

Annual Goal: Student will demonstrate appropriate social responding and reciprocity across 3 familiar social games and 3 familiar songs in his preschool classroom, 8/10 opportunities.

Explanatory Note: Follow-up goals and objectives could further expand the number of activities that the child finds enjoyable. In addition, an appropriate next step would be to gradually introduce peers into the interactive, reciprocal games involving movement and song.

Sharing

Sample PLP for a four-year-old student with NLD: According to clinical observation and teacher report, student is able to engage in parallel play activities but has a great deal of difficulty sharing toys with peers. Her speech-language pathologist reports that when engaging in water or sand play activities, student often gets upset when she has to relinquish a preferred toy. These difficulties affect her ability to participate in group and play activities in her preschool classroom, and cause her peers to avoid playing with her.

Goal/Objective Templates Based on PLP

Short-Term Objective 1:   Given 2 neutral toys and a 3-minute timer, student will pass the toy to an adult for 1 minute, 3/5 opportunities in a 10-minute sustained play interaction at a sand or water table, given a direct verbal cue to share, physical assistance, if needed, and praise for relinquishing the toy.

Short-Term Objective 2:   Given 1 preferred and 2 neutral toys and a 5-minute timer, student will pass the preferred toy to an adult for 2 minutes, 4/5 opportunities in a 15-minute sustained play interaction at a sand or water table, given indirect verbal cue ("What is it time to do?") paired with upturned palm, and praise for relinquishing the toy.

Short-Term Objective 3:   Given a 5-minute timer and 3–4 preferred and non-preferred toys, student will pass each toy to 1 or another peer when prompted by the adult to share, 4/5 opportunities in a 20-minute sustained play interaction at a sand or water table, given expectant waiting and praise for relinquishing the toy.

Annual Goal: Given a 20-minute structured play interaction in the preschool classroom, student will share 4–5 play objects with 1 or 2 peers, with indirect cueing and facilitation by an adult, as needed.

Turn-Taking

Sample PLP for an eight-year-old student with ADHD: Student enjoys playing board games with other children; however, because of her inattention and impulsivity she has difficulty remembering to take her turn. This is particularly problematic in games where there are double turns, or where one must sometimes miss a turn. This behavior frustrates her peers and interferes with student's ability to develop social relationships in her classroom.

Goal/Objective Templates Based on PLP

Short-Term Objective 1:   Given direct instruction in the use of a turn marker (for example, a circle made out of construction paper with the words *my turn* written on it), student will take turns with a peer in a two-person game by moving the turn marker back and forth at the appropriate times, for 70% of turns per 15-minute period, given direct verbal cues to use the turn marker.

Short-Term Objective 2:   Given a turn marker, student will take turns with a peer in a 2-person game by moving the turn marker back and forth at the appropriate times, for 80% of turns per 20-minute period, given indirect verbal cues regarding the turn marker.

Short-Term Objective 3:   Given a turn marker, student will take turns with a peer in a 3-person game by moving the turn marker at the appropriate time, 80% of turns in a 30-minute period, given gestural cues to the turn marker.

Annual Goal: Given a turn marker, student will take turns with 1–4 peers, during 2-, 3-, and 4-person games, 90% of turns in a 30–45 minute period, independently.

Social Participation in Games with Rules

Sample PLP for a twelve-year-old student with ED: According to his PE teacher, student enjoys sports and group games, but he often becomes extremely competitive and angry if his team does not win. This can lead to elopement from school or aggressive behavior, which threatens his safety and that of others. Because of student's difficulties, he is often the last player chosen by his peers to be on a team.

Goal/Objective Templates Based on PLP

Short-Term Objective 1:   Given direct instruction and practice in 3 specific appropriate reactions to losing a game, and the use of a rehearsal strategy (for example, cognitive picture rehearsal or a social story), student will apply an appropriate reaction in each of 5 role-play scenarios involving the loss of a game with 1 peer, 3/5 opportunities, with direct verbal and manual sign cues to "stop and think" before responding.

Short-Term Objective 2: Given the use of a rehearsal strategy, student will demonstrate maintenance of skills by reacting appropriately in the previous role-plays, and apply an appropriate reaction in each of 5 new role-play scenarios involving the loss of a game with 2–3 peers, 4/5 opportunities, with indirect verbal or manual sign cues.

Short-Term Objective 3: Given the use of a rehearsal strategy, and the presence of an informed adult, student will react appropriately to the loss of actual games with a variety of peers across a 2-week period of structured PE activities, 80% of the time, with minimal gestural cues.

Annual Goal: Given the use of a rehearsal strategy prior to participation, student will react appropriately to the loss of actual games with a variety of peers in structured PE and unstructured recess activities, 90% of the time, independently.

Following "Unwritten" Social Rules

Sample PLP for a fifteen-year-old student with NLD: Student is described as "very social" by her parents and teachers, at least in terms of her desire to engage with peers. Despite this, her lack of knowledge of the unwritten rules of social discourse impedes her ability to interact with others appropriately. When conversing, she is frequently observed to stand too close to adults and peers, which causes them to feel uncomfortable. These difficulties affect student's ability to establish relationships with peers and to function effectively in social situations in classroom or extracurricular settings.

Goal/Objective Template Based on PLP

Short-Term Objective 1: Given direct instruction and practice, and a concrete visual cue (for example, tape on the floor), student will maintain an appropriate social distance when speaking to another person in a series of role-play situations for 3 minutes, 100% of the time, given intermittent social praise as a reminder and to reinforce appropriate behavior.

Short-Term Objective 2: Given a directive to maintain social distance and a less direct visual cue (for example, outstretched arm of conversational partner only if student attempts to stand too close), student will maintain an appropriate social distance when speaking to another person in a series of role-play situations for 5 minutes, given intermittent social praise as a reminder and to reinforce appropriate behavior, with no more than 3 reminders (outstretched arm).

Short-Term Objective 3: Given a specific prior verbal reminder, student will maintain an appropriate social distance when speaking to another person in a series of role-play situations for 10 minutes, with intermittent social praise as a reminder and to reinforce appropriate behavior, with no more than 1 reminder.

Annual Goal: Student will maintain an appropriate social distance when speaking to another person for 10 minutes without reminders or cues.

"Sizing Up" Social Situations

Sample PLP for a ten-year-old student with ADD and NLD: According to his teacher, student appears motivated to interact with peers, as judged by his frequent attempts to interact in the classroom setting. Despite his interest, however, he is unsuccessful in these attempts. His difficulty appears to stem from a lack of social understanding of nonverbal signals, which is complicated by his problems in sustaining attention. These difficulties are reportedly off-putting to his peers, and hence negatively affect student's ability to derive benefit from typical peer models in his inclusive classroom setting.

Short-Term Objective 1: Given direct instruction and 10 observational vignettes containing exaggerated cues, student will "size up" a variety of social situations by selecting appropriate explanations of them in a multiple-choice format, 80% of the time, given direct verbal and gestural cues.

Short-Term Objective 2: Given additional instruction and 5 new and 10 previously viewed observational vignettes, student will "size up" a variety of social situations by providing verbal explanations of them, at an 80% level of correctness, given indirect verbal or gestural cues.

Short-Term Objective 3: Given a Social Story™ and manual-sign cues, as needed, student will demonstrate social understanding by generating appropriate social responses in contextually relevant role-play situations, with 1 adult and 1 peer, 90% of the time, given minimal gestural cues.

Annual Goal: Student will demonstrate understanding of social information/ events in structured situations in the classroom by exhibiting social behavior appropriate to the context, 80% of opportunities, independently.

Explanatory Note: For additional information on Social Stories™ (Gray, 2010), see Appendix B.

CONTENT AREA: THEORY OF MIND

Perspective Taking: Determining/Inferring Mental State

Sample PLP for a thirteen-year-old student with ED: According to her teacher, student manifests strengths in vocabulary, spelling, and reading decoding, and does well in several academic subjects. However, her teacher and parents report that she becomes highly agitated when others don't agree with her. As a result, she is often argumentative both at home and in school. Her accuracy rate on the *Test of Problem Solving—Adolescent* is 40% for questions that involve perspective taking. Because of these difficulties, student has problems making friends and interacting with both adult and peers in an appropriate manner.

Goal/Objective Templates Based on PLP

Short-Term Objective 1:   Given direct instruction and modeling in making predictions about mental states (for example, angry, sad, anxious, and so on), and 10 videotaped vignettes involving exaggerated emotional cues and stop-action pausing to allow prediction, student will select the card from a group of 3 presented that best predicts the emotional reaction that will occur when the action is resumed, for 7/10 vignettes, given direct and indirect verbal cues.

Short-Term Objective 2:   Given 10 new videotaped vignettes involving typically depicted emotional cues and stop-action pausing to allow prediction, student will select the card from a group of 4 presented that best predicts the emotional reaction that will occur when the action is resumed, for 8/10 vignettes, given indirect verbal cues.

Note that moving from the exaggerated cues specified in Short-Term Objective 1 to more normalized ones is an excellent way of fading back prompts and demonstrating progress.

Short-Term Objective 3:   Given a series of social situations (for example, a mean remark by a classmate, losing a class vote on an activity, and so on), student will predict the emotional response that will be depicted in structured role-plays acted out by informed peers in the speech-language therapy room, for 8/10 vignettes, given gestural cues.

Annual Goal: Student will select a role-play scenario and act out an appropriate response to it with at least 2 peers, for 8/10 vignettes, given expectant waiting.

Explanatory Note: An excellent follow-up annual goal to this one would be to have the student switch roles in situations where two or more emotional reactions may be appropriate.

Sample PLP for a nine-year-old student with NLD: According to formal assessment, clinical observation, and teacher report, student is able to recognize some of the more obvious emotions in pictures (for example, happy, sad, angry), but does not acknowledge these emotions when others display them in day-to-day activities. In addition, he does not appear to connect the emotion with the event or circumstance that caused it. These deficits compromise overall sense making, and make it difficult for him to make inferences and predictions about another person's behavior.

Goal/Objective Templates Based on PLP

Short-Term Objective 1:   Given prior direct instruction and several examples, and 10 paragraphs, each of which contains a picture depicting a character's emotional reaction to an event, student will answer questions regarding *how* the person feels, and *why* the character feels that way, 7/10 opportunities, given direct verbal cues. (Consider, for example, a paragraph concerning two children playing baseball and a broken window. The boy holding the baseball bat looks really sad. *Questions/actions:* 1. How do you think the boy feels? [*Answer:* Unhappy.]. 2. Why do you think he feels that way? [*Answer:* Because he broke the window].)

Short-Term Objective 2:   Given 10 new paragraphs, each of which contains a picture depicting a character's emotional reaction to an event, student will answer questions regarding *how* the person feels; *why* the character feels that way; and *how* that might make Mom or Dad feel, 8/10 opportunities for the first 2 questions, and 6/10 for the third question, given direct and indirect verbal and gestural cues. (In this example, the third question might be: "How do you think Mom or Dad will feel about the broken window?" *Answer:* Angry.)

Short-Term Objective 3:   Given 10 new paragraphs, each of which contains a picture depicting a character's emotional reaction to an event, student will tell *how* the person feels; *why* the character feels that way; and *how* that might make Mom or Dad feel, 8/10 opportunities for each question, given minimal gestural cues as needed.

Annual Goal: Student will predict how characters in stories feel in response to events and how those events impact others, 80% of the time, across academic tasks, given expectant waiting or indirect verbal cues as needed.

Sample PLP for a twelve-year-old with ED: Student demonstrates strengths in vocabulary and reading decoding that mask her significant difficulty with perspective taking. She is very unilateral in her thinking, and gives no credence to anyone's perspective/opinion but her own. This is particularly apparent in situations in which multiple perspectives over the same issue might occur. Student's insistence on "her way or the highway" is negatively affecting both her grades and her social relationships. (Teaching tip 10 at the end of this chapter provides detailed information on how to teach the perspective-taking skills addressed in the following short-term objectives and annual goal.)

Short-Term Objective 1:   Given direct instruction/examples on what is meant by perspective taking, and 10 story scenarios in which 2 characters feel *differently* about the *same* situation (for example, happy or sad about a baseball game), student will demonstrate understanding of the different perspectives by selecting appropriate reasons for the emotional states depicted, from a multiple-choice format, at a 70% level of correctness, given direct verbal cues and explanation regarding incorrect responses.

Short-Term Objective 2:   Given 10 previous and 5 new story scenarios in which 2 characters feel differently about the same situation, student will demonstrate understanding of the different perspectives by stating the reasons for the emotional states in the previous 10 scenarios, and by selecting appropriate reasons from a multiple-choice format for the 5 new scenarios, at an 80% level of correctness, given indirect verbal cues and explanation, as needed.

Short-Term Objective 3:   Given contrived events acted out in structured role-plays, student will demonstrate understanding of each character's different perspective regarding the same situation by selecting the *best* reason for the emotional state depicted from a list of *reasonable possibilities* in a multiple-choice format and stating the reason for her choice, 80% for each, given gestural cues.

Annual Goal: Student will demonstrate understanding of characters' different perspectives by stating the reasons for them across academic subjects, where appropriate (for example, English class, history, and so on), 90% of the time, with minimal indirect verbal cueing.

Sample PLP for a sixteen-year-old student with ED: Cafeteria and hallway monitors have corroborated the complaints of many of student's peers that he engages in unprovoked bullying behavior. Most of the incidents that occur surround circumstances in which student doesn't get his own way. His responses on *Test of Problem Solving—Adolescent* indicate that he has difficulty with perspective taking, and as such, he has difficulty determining the effect of his behavior on others. Student's perspective-taking problems cause him to react aggressively to peers when they do not go along with his wishes. In addition, his teachers speculate that his lack of insight into his perspective-taking problems cause him to blame others for their perceived rejection of him, creating a vicious cycle of rejection and blame.

Short-Term Objective 1: Given direct instruction and examples of what is meant by "off-putting" (bullying) and "friend-making" behavior, student will select from a list of 20 remarks those that typify friend-making (appropriate) behavior, at an 80% level of accuracy, given indirect verbal cues and explanation regarding incorrect responses.

Short-Term Objective 2: Given 10 written scenarios, student will generate 10 appropriate responses to them and give the reason for his choices, at an 80% level of accuracy, given expectant waiting or minimal gestural cueing as needed.

Short-Term Objective 3: Given 10 open-ended role-play scenarios with an adult, student will act out appropriate responses to them, across at least 2 turns, at an 80% level of accuracy, given expectant waiting or gestural cues as needed, and later explain the reasons for his choice of behavioral responses.

Annual Goal: Given 10 open ended role-play scenarios with 1 or 2 peers, student will act out appropriate responses to them, across at least 3–4 turns, at an 80% level of accuracy, independently.

CONTENT AREA: PLAY SKILLS DEVELOPMENT

Expanding Actions on Objects

Sample PLP for a six-year-old student with ASD: According to his parents and teacher, once student is interested in a particular toy, he can derive enjoyment from it. They state, however, that he is very resistant to new things. When left to his own devices, he will often engage in self-stimulatory behavior with toys. He particularly likes shiny objects, and will often hold them up to his eyes. He also spins the wheels on toy cars. In addition, student will only attempt to play with 2 of the items in the play corner, and protests when presented with any other objects. These difficulties affect student's ability to understand core concepts and interfere with his ability to engage with peers.

Goal/Objective Templates Based on PLP

Short-Term Objective 1:   Given 2 toys that contain elements of interest to the student (for example, shiny, or with components that spin), and demonstration and modeling, student will incorporate at least one new action into his play repertoire, for 3 instances per toy, given physical assistance and direct verbal cues as needed.

Short-Term Objective 2:   Given 2 previous and 2 new toys that contain elements of interest to the student, and demonstration and modeling of new actions, student will demonstrate maintenance of the previously learned play behavior and expand upon it by adding 1 new action, and will incorporate at least 2 new actions into his play repertoire with the new toys, for 3 instances per toy, given direct verbal or physical assistance, as needed.

Short-Term Objective 3:   Given 4 previously used toys, student will incorporate at least 2 new actions into his toy play for each toy, for 4 instances per toy given a manual sign or gesture cue.

Annual Goal: Given 4 new toys that are very similar to the ones previously given, student will spontaneously generate at least 2 new actions into his toy play, for 5 instances per toy, given indirect verbal cues (for example, "I wonder if the car goes down the hill.")

Expanding Play Stages

Sample PLP for a three-year-old student with ASD: Student is beginning to expand her play repertoire during solitary play activities; however, she is not yet comfortable with the proximity of peers, as evidenced by her moving to an isolated corner of the classroom when peers approach her. Student's lack of comfort with parallel play keeps her isolated and on the periphery of classroom activities.

Goal/Objective Templates Based on PLP

Short-Term Objective 1:   Given a sand or water table, and highly preferred toys or containers, student will demonstrate her comfort level in the proximity of peers by playing in parallel fashion across from 1 adult and 1 peer, for a 5-minute play period, 7/10 opportunities, given verbal praise and adult facilitation as needed.

Short-Term Objective 2:   Given a sand or water table, and both highly and moderately preferred toys or containers, student will demonstrate her comfort level in the proximity of peers by playing in parallel fashion across from 1 and alongside another peer, for a 10-minute play period, 8/10 opportunities, given verbal praise and adult facilitation as needed.

Short-Term Objective 3: Given a sand or water table, and both highly and moderately preferred toys/containers, student will demonstrate associative play skills by accepting from 2 peers highly preferred toys/containers, during a 15-minute play period, 8/10 opportunities, given indirect verbal cues and praise.

Annual Goal: Given a sand or water table and a variety of toys/containers, student will demonstrate associative play skills by handing to and/or accepting from 2 peers toys/containers, during a 15-minute play period, 9/10 opportunities, given gestural cues and praise.

Explanatory Note: The short-term objectives above move the child along the continuum from solitary play to parallel play, and finally to associative play (play levels based on Mildred Parton's stages of play). The next step would be to write an annual goal and short-term objectives for rudimentary cooperative play.

Early Interactive/Cooperative Play

Sample PLP for a four-year-old student with ADD/ADHD: According to both formal and informal testing, student manifests strengths in academic areas such as knowing her colors, shapes, and numbers. She is extremely active, and reportedly "flits" from thing to thing. Her parents report that she enjoys "roughhouse" play and other high-intensity activities. Student often approaches her peers in her preschool classroom, but her impulsive and sometimes aggressive behavior often causes her peers to avoid playing with her. In addition, she often leaves play activities abruptly because another activity has captured her attention.

Goal/Objective Templates Based on PLP

Short-Term Objective 1: Given motivating, developmentally appropriate high-intensity activities, student will engage in reciprocal play interactions with at least 1 peer by performing the actions appropriate to the activity, for 4 minutes across 3 activities given adult facilitation and direct verbal cues. (High-intensity activities can include the following: playing *Ring-Around-the-Rosie; Row, Row, Row Your Boat;* and *London Bridge Is Falling Down* with a partner; seesaw interactions; and similar activities.)

Short-Term Objective 2: Given motivating, developmentally appropriate high-intensity activities, student will engage in reciprocal play interactions with at least 2 peers by performing the actions appropriate to the activity, for 7 minutes, across 3 previous and 3 new activities, given adult facilitation and gestural cues.

Short-Term Objective 3:   Given motivating, developmentally appropriate activities that are of medium to low intensity (for example, playing with a toy, sand/water table, and so on), student will engage in reciprocal play interactions with at least 2 peers by performing the actions appropriate to the activity, for 5–7 minutes across 3 activities, given adult facilitation and indirect verbal and gestural cues.

Annual Goal: Given motivating, developmentally appropriate activities that are of high, medium, or low intensity, student will engage in reciprocal play interactions with at least 2–3 peers by performing the actions appropriate to the activity, for a minimum of 7–10 minutes (depending upon intensity level), across 10 activities, given minimal gestural cues.

Cooperative Play: Using Social Scripts

Sample PLP for a five-year-old student with ASD: Student is extremely verbal with adults, particularly if talking about trains—his current abiding interest. His parents have expressed concern, however, because when they take him to the park or to visit other children, he shows no interest, whatsoever, in what they are doing. Attempts to get him to join in games have been met with a great deal of resistance. These difficulties prevent student from participating fully in kindergarten activities with peers.

Goal/Objective Templates Based on PLP

Short-Term Objective 1:   Given a social script involving a pretend train trip, rules for playing, props, and an assigned role, student will perform the actions required, with at least 5–6 peers, for a 10-minute period, 4/5 opportunities, at a proficiency level of 3 (out of 5 possible), given direct verbal and picture cues.

Explanatory Notes:

- The selection of a train-related scenario is based upon the child's "abiding interest" in trains, as such interest is likely to provide the motivation to participate in the role-play.

- Because this type of skill development lends itself to qualitative assessment, a Likert-type rating scale with specified behaviors can yield important information regarding progress. For example (behavioral descriptors may be changed to suit the particular situation):

- 1= No response

- 2= Minimal response (5 minutes or less)

- 3= Moderate response (minimum of 10 minutes; passive participation)

- 4= Very good response (Minimum of 15–20 minutes; good affective response)

- 5= Excellent response (25 or more minutes; active participation; comments/expanded repertoire)

Short-Term Objective 2:   Given a social script involving a pretend train trip, rules for playing, props, and a choice of roles, student will select a role and perform the actions required with at least 6–7 peers, for at least 15–20 minutes, 4/5 opportunities, at a proficiency level of 4, given indirect verbal and picture cues.

Short-Term Objective 3:   Given a pretend train trip scenario and rules for participation, props, and a choice of roles, student will select a role and perform the actions required with at least 8–10 peers, for at least 20–25 minutes, 4/5 opportunities, at a proficiency level of 4, given minimal gestural cues.

Annual Goal: Given a pretend train trip scenario and rules for participation, props, and a choice of roles, student will select a role and perform the actions required with at least 8–10 peers, for at least 25–30 minutes, 4/5 opportunities, at a proficiency level of 5, given minimal indirect verbal cues to facilitate and expand play interaction (for example, "I wonder if that food car is open yet").

Explanatory Note: Future goals may address the expansion of this type of cooperative play activity into other content areas (for example, playing restaurant).

CONTENT AREA: LEISURE SKILL DEVELOPMENT

Sample PLP for a sixteen-year-old student with moderately severe autism: Student works very hard in both his highly structured vocational class and job site. He has difficulty, however, during unstructured time (that is, the 15-minute break that he is required to take). His parents also report that student becomes agitated and restless when he is at home and time is not structured for him. During these times, he is prone to engaging in self-stimulatory behavior. Difficulties managing unstructured time impact student's ability to function effectively across home, school, and work settings.

Goal/Objective Templates Based on PLP

It is recommended that an ecological inventory be taken in order to develop a list of leisure activities that the student finds pleasurable.

Short-Term Objective 1: Given a group of leisure activities that the student finds pleasurable and a visual timer (for example, *Time Timer*), student will choose an activity from a visual array of 2 choices, and participate in it, for 5–7 minutes, given direct verbal and gestural cues to the timer in the classroom setting. (See Appendix B for ordering information on the *Time Timer*).

Short-Term Objective 2: Given a group of leisure activities that the student finds pleasurable and a visual timer, student will choose an activity from a visual array of 3 choices, and participate in it, for 8–10 minutes, given indirect verbal and gestural cues to the timer in the classroom setting.

Short-Term Objective 3: Given a group of leisure activities that the student finds pleasurable and a visual timer, student will choose an activity from a visual array of 3 choices, and participate in it, for 15 minutes, given gestural cues to the timer in the classroom and vocational settings.

Annual Goal: Student will select a break activity from a visual array of 3 choices and participate in it, for 15 minutes, independently, across settings.

GENERAL TEACHING TIPS AND STRATEGIES FOR SOCIAL-COGNITION, PLAY, AND LEISURE SKILL DEVELOPMENT

1. Use motivating, developmentally appropriate toys (for younger students), and developmentally appropriate activities (for older students).

2. Work within functional, naturalistic contexts whenever possible, to help facilitate the generalization of skills.

3. Provide direct instruction to students and use demonstration and modeling, whenever possible.

4. Repetition of social skills, play, and leisure activities over time is critical both to learning and generalizing these important skills.

5. Train paraprofessionals to work on social skills, play, and leisure skills in classroom, recess, resource room, and extracurricular environments to promote generalization across people, activities, and settings.

6. Concretize the abstract concept of turn-taking by using a turn marker (such as a circle with the words *my turn* written on it).

7. Provide much-needed social interaction practice for students in nonthreatening environments through the use of structured role-plays.

8. Frequently point out the emotions of others in naturally occurring situations to help students connect emotional states to activities and events.

9. "Code" the thoughts of students with ASD and NLD in situations involving high emotion (both positive and negative), so that they can begin to make connections between their external behavior and their emotions/feelings.

10. Create a perspective-taking game in which two characters (Sammy and Suzie) react differently to the same situation. Draw faces on a chalk or laminate board, where one character has a smile while the other one has a frown. Write the reasons for their disparate reactions on index cards that the student has to match to the emotional state depicted (happy or sad). Consider the following scenario: *Situation:* "It's raining. Suzie is frowning, but Sammy is smiling." Direct the student to find out the reasons why Suzie and Sammy feel differently about the same situation (the rain) by having him or her pick a card and match it to the character portraying the appropriate mental state. Sample reasons could include the following:

    • Suzie was supposed to go on a picnic, but the picnic has been cancelled because it's raining. (That's why Suzie is sad.)

    • Sammy was supposed to mow the lawn, but because it's raining, he won't be able to do it. (That's why Sammy is happy.)

    Give the student many opportunities to engage in perspective-taking activities by fabricating several additional scenarios.

11. Keep uppermost in mind that play and leisure skills must be enjoyable to the student if they are to qualify under the category of play and

leisure. "Forcing" enjoyment because it happens to be play or leisure time distorts the properties of both.

12. Consider using social scripts, picture rehearsal (Groden, LeVasseur, Diller, and Cautela, 2001), and Social Stories™ (Gray, 2010) to promote social understanding.

14

EXECUTIVE FUNCTION: THE PINNACLE OF COGNITIVE DEVELOPMENT

"Knowledge is of no value unless you put it into practice."

—Anton Chekov

RATIONALE FOR INCLUDING SKILL CATEGORY

Executive function (EF) skills encompass the following areas of functioning:

- Emotional regulation/control (Dawson and Guare, 2009)
- Attending
- Mental planning
- Task initiation
- Transitioning

- Goal-directed persistence (the ability to persist with a task until it is completed) (Dawson and Guare, 2009)

- Impulse control

- Flexibility in thought and action

- Working memory (the ability to keep plans and goals "online")

- Self-monitoring

- Time management

- Organization

Executive function difficulties affect students with a variety of disabilities, including ASD (Ozonoff, 1997; Pennington, Bennetto, McAleer, and Roberts, 1996); ADD/ADHD (Barkley, 2006; Dawson and Guare, 2009; Rief, 2005); NLD (Mamen, 2007; Tanguay, 2001); and some manifestations of ED (Garcia Coll, Kagan, and Resnick, 1984). Since EF deficits affect mental flexibility and adaptive functioning, and because competence in executive function skills is crucial to higher-level thinking and independence, it may well be said that it is in the area of executive functioning where "the rubber meets the road" for most of the conditions covered in this book. Specifically, it is the EF system that oversees organized, goal-directed behavior, so essential to independent functioning and overall success. Importantly, while EF deficits are more readily apparent in older and more-able students, they are nevertheless important areas of development in younger and less-able students with these conditions. Indeed, the roots of EF take hold in early childhood wherein the child learns how to regulate him- or herself, and eventually, others. Hence, given the importance of the EF system to overall functioning and independence, IEP teams are urged to give specific attention to the skill areas subsumed within it for students with the disabilities covered in this book. This is especially important because deficits in EF are often mistaken for noncompliance or laziness.

PRESENT LEVELS OF PERFORMANCE FOR EXECUTIVE FUNCTION

The PLP for executive function should include

- A statement indicating the student's strengths in executive functioning, particularly as they relate to academic achievement and functional performance

- A statement on the student's weaknesses in executive functioning, particularly as they relate to academic achievement, functional performance, and priority educational needs for the coming year

- A statement of how the student's deficits in executive functioning impact his or her involvement and progress in the general curriculum (or for preschool children, in appropriate activities)

- The sources of the statements in the PLP (optional)

- Any additional information that can enable the PLP to fulfill its two important functions: (1) to serve as the basis for generating need-based individualized IEP goals and objectives, and (2) to serve as the standard by which to judge student performance and progress

CONTENT AREA: TRANSITIONING

Using a Daily Schedule

Sample PLP for a twelve-year-old student with moderate ASD and S/LI: According to clinical observation and teacher report, when student is involved in an activity he is able to function adequately. The amount of time it takes him to "settle in," however, is often a problem, as student has difficulty transitioning from one activity to another, especially when the upcoming activity is unexpected or undesired. He also becomes upset when unanticipated events disrupt his routine. These difficulties interfere with the initiation of academic tasks and transitioning from one activity or class to another.

Goal/Objective Templates Based on PLP

Short Term Objective 1: Given a daily visual schedule and direct verbal cues to check it at transition points, student will demonstrate the ability to transition from activity to activity by: (1) obtaining the appropriate picture card; (2) moving to the appropriate place; and (3) returning the picture card to the "finished" box/envelope at the conclusion of the activity for 70% of activities, given additional direct verbal/gestural cues for each step, as needed.

Short-Term Objective 2: Given a daily visual schedule and indirect verbal cues (for example, "What is it time to do?") at transition points, student will demonstrate the ability to transition from activity to activity by: (1) obtaining the appropriate picture card; (2) moving to the appropriate place; and (3) returning the picture card to the "finished" box/envelope at the conclusion of the activity for 80% of activities, given minimal gestural cues (for example, pointing to schedule), as needed.

Short-Term Objective 3: Given a daily visual schedule, student will demonstrate the ability to transition from activity to activity by: (1) obtaining the appropriate picture card; (2) moving to the appropriate place; and (3) returning the picture card to the "finished" box/envelope at the conclusion of the activity for 90% of activities, given expectant waiting.

Annual Goal: Given a daily visual schedule, student will demonstrate the ability to transition from activity to activity by: (1) obtaining the appropriate picture card; (2) moving to the appropriate place; and (3) returning the picture card to the "finished" box/envelope at the conclusion of the activity for all activities, independently.

Explanatory Note: Direct verbal cues were provided in only the first short-term objective, with gradually decreasing prompt levels thereafter. This is intended to foster independence by moving from a higher-prompt level (for example, "Check your schedule") to a lower-prompt level (for example, "What is it time to do?") and so forth.

Using a Planner

Sample PLP for a fourteen-year-old student with NLD: According to informal observation and teacher report, student has difficulty knowing which class to go to in her rotating high school schedule. As a result, she often goes to the wrong classroom and is late for her actual class. This disrupts her classmates and causes her to miss the homework turn-in time and important classroom instructions, which negatively impacts her grades.

Goal/Objective Templates Based on PLP

Short-Term Objective 1: Given a written daily schedule in a planning book, student will demonstrate the ability to transition from class to class on time for 70% of classes, given 5 minutes of lead time and direct verbal cues at the end of each class to check her schedule.

Short-Term Objective 2: Given a daily planner, student will demonstrate the ability to transition from class to class on time for 80% of classes, given 2 minutes of lead time and indirect verbal cues at the end of each class (for example, "What do you need to check?").

Short-Term Objective 3: Given a daily planner, student will demonstrate the ability to transition from class to class on time for 90% of classes, given 2 minutes of lead time and expectant waiting regarding the schedule.

Annual Goal: Given a daily planner, student will demonstrate the ability to transition from class to class on time for 90% of classes, independently.

Explanatory Note: Although the prompt to check the schedule is gradually faded for this fourteen-year-old student, use of the planner (underlying condition) is not, because it serves as an accommodation to enable successful transitioning.

CONTENT AREA: GOAL-DIRECTED BEHAVIOR

Task Initiation

Sample PLP for a five-year-old student with ED: Student has no difficulty participating in classroom activities he enjoys; however, when his teacher asks him to participate in those that he does not enjoy, student engages in various avoidance behaviors (for example, moving to another part of the room; ignoring the directive). When his teacher approaches him, student often says that he will "do it in a minute." After several reminders, and a threatened loss of privileges, student is able to complete the task in a satisfactory manner, but the reminders interfere with completion of assignments and are disruptive to his classmates.

Goal/Objective Templates Based on PLP

Short-Term Objective 1:   Given a directive to engage in a nonpreferred task, student will respond appropriately within 30 seconds and see the task through to completion (with verbal praise along the way), given a maximum of 2 reminders and the use of an immediate reward system (for example, check mark for initiation; sticker for task completion).

Short-Term Objective 2:   Given a directive to engage in a nonpreferred task, student will respond appropriately within 20 seconds and see the task through to completion (with verbal praise along the way), given a maximum of 1 reminder and the use of an immediate reward system (for example, check mark for initiation; sticker for task completion).

Short-Term Objective 3:   Given a directive to engage in a nonpreferred task, student will respond appropriately in a timely manner (within 10 seconds) and see the task through to completion, given verbal praise for initiation, and the use of a delayed reward system (for example, sticker at the end of the day for task completion).

Annual Goal: Student will respond to directives to engage in nonpreferred tasks in a timely manner (within 10 seconds) and see them through to completion, with verbal praise for doing so.

Explanatory Note: In the early stages of work on this executive skill, the length of time expected for the student to work on nonpreferred tasks should be relatively brief to increase the likelihood of task initiation. As performance improves, time periods may be gradually extended.

Persistence Toward Task Completion

Sample PLP for a fourteen-year-old student with ADD: Although achievement testing demonstrates that student is able to perform academic tasks at grade level, she often does not sustain effort long enough to complete academic assignments. Currently, assignments are only completed when student's teacher or parents remind her multiple times to return to the task at hand. Even with reminders, both classroom worksheets and homework assignments are often incomplete and marred by careless errors or unacceptably messy workmanship. Student's performance negatively impacts her grades and causes her and her teachers and parents significant frustration.

Goal/Objective Templates Based on PLP

Short-Term Objective 1:   Given a worksheet broken down into 3 parts, and a 3-minute mini break between each part, student will complete all of the items on the worksheet accurately and neatly for 4/5 worksheets, with a maximum of 3 reminders to maintain effort/attend to task.

Short-Term Objective 2:   Given a worksheet broken down into 3 parts, and a 3-minute mini break between each part, student will complete all of the items on the worksheet accurately and neatly, for 4/5 worksheets, with a maximum of 1 reminder to maintain effort/attend to task.

Short-Term Objective 3:   Given a time-management checklist with mini breaks at set intervals, student will complete all of the items on the worksheet accurately and neatly for 5/5 worksheets, with a maximum of 1 reminder to maintain effort/attend to task.

Annual Goal: Given a time-management checklist, student will complete all the items on all class worksheets assigned, accurately and independently.

CONTENT AREA: SELF-MONITORING

Emotional Regulation

Sample PLP for a sixteen-year-old student with ED: According to his teachers, student is able to manage his emotions well in calm and structured situations.

In unstructured social situations, or when a peer says or does something that he does not like, student will often become aggressive and have difficulty controlling his anger. Student's anger-management issues interfere with peer relationships and pose safety concerns for his classmates. They are also impacting academic performance.

Goal/Objective Templates Based on PLP

Short-Term Objective 1: Given instructional support, student will identify 5 situations that make him angry; generate 5 strategies designed to reduce his impulsive responses; and incorporate the strategies into an anger deceleration protocol.

Short-Term Objective 2: Given an anger deceleration protocol (for example, a scale with student-generated strategies for reducing anger), student will employ appropriate anger-management strategies in 5 peer-conflict role-plays, 8/10 opportunities, given direct and indirect verbal cues to use the protocol.

Short-Term Objective 3: Given an anger deceleration protocol, student will employ the appropriate anger-management strategies in 3 new and 5 previously performed peer-conflict role-plays, 8/10 opportunities, given gestural cues to use the protocol.

Short-Term Objective 4: Given an anger deceleration protocol and supervised, contrived anger-provoking situations in the school setting, student will employ appropriate anger-management strategies, 8/10 opportunities, given direct verbal cues to consult the protocol and verbal praise for doing so.

Annual Goal: Given an anger deceleration protocol, student will demonstrate the use of appropriate anger-management strategies in 8/10 opportunities in classroom situations that are anger-provoking, with gestural cues to consult the protocol, as needed.

Impulse Control

Sample PLP for a four-year-old student with ADHD: Despite student's strengths in vocabulary development, spelling, and reading decoding, her teacher reports that she is "extremely impulsive," citing as an example her habit of constantly blurting out questions and comments during morning circle. According to the teacher, student's difficulty controlling her impulses is beginning to take its toll on her classmates, as evidenced by their reactions to her disruptions. This problem impedes student's ability to participate appropriately in many of the classroom group activities, and interferes with her ability to establish relationships with peers.

Goal/Objective Templates Based on PLP

Short-Term Objective 1:   Given direct instruction in the use of a visual cue (for example, red "light" means time to be quiet; green "light" means it's okay to talk), student will demonstrate improvement in impulse control by reducing the number of interruptions during 1 classroom group activity (for example, morning circle) by 60% over baseline, given direct verbal directives to attend to the (traffic light) visual cue.

Short-Term Objective 2:   Given a visual cue, student will demonstrate improvement in impulse control by reducing the number of interruptions during 2 classroom group activities by 70% over baseline for each activity, given indirect verbal cues (for example, "What color is the light?").

Short-Term Objective 3:   Given a visual cue, student will demonstrate improvement in impulse control by reducing the number of interruptions during 3 classroom group activities by 80% over baseline for each activity, given gestures to attend to the visual cue.

Annual Goal: Given a visual cue, student will demonstrate improvement in impulse control by reducing the number of interruptions across all classroom group activities, 80% over baseline for each activity, with expectant waiting or gestural cues as needed.

Explanatory Note: Control of impulsivity is very difficult for students with EF deficits, particularly at young ages, given their problems with distractibility and working memory. Hence, when they are verbally told to raise their hands, they usually do so—only to forget a few moments later when they have something else to say. For this reason, impulse control should be considered a work in progress, in which the visual cue serves as a working memory support, as opposed to a prompt to be immediately faded. Think of it this way: *verbally rendered directives to "raise your hand" go in one ear and out the other, while visual cues provide a stable and lasting reminder.*

Managing Homework Assignments

Sample PLP for a fifteen-year-old student with NLD: Student's teachers and parents report that he has considerable difficulty completing homework assignments because he often forgets to bring home the necessary materials.

In addition, even when he does complete assignments, he often forgets to take them to school or hand them in. These difficulties affect student's ability to meet academic requirements and cause teachers and peers to view him as lazy and disorganized.

Goal/Objective Templates Based on PLP

Short-Term Objective 1:   Given a home-school homework checklist (see the example below), student will complete and hand in homework assignments across all academic subjects, 70% of opportunities, given direct verbal cues to use his checklist and reward points for doing so.

Short-Term Objective 2:   Given a home-school homework checklist, student will complete and hand in homework assignments across all academic subjects 80% of opportunities, given indirect verbal cues to use his checklist and reward points for doing so.

Short-Term Objective 3:   Given a home-school homework checklist, student will complete and hand in homework assignments across all academic subjects 90% of opportunities, independently, given verbal praise for doing so.

Annual Goal: Student will independently use a home-school homework checklist to complete and hand in homework assignments across all academic subjects 100% of the time.

Sample Homework Checklist:

- Copy homework assignment.
- Obtain materials needed and put them in backpack.
- Complete assignments at home.
- Place assignments in appropriate homework folders and put in backpack.
- Hand in completed homework assignments.

Explanatory Note: Many teachers make the mistake of fading back organizational supports such as checklists in their attempt to foster independence. Because executive functioning is a deficit area in students with the types of conditions addressed in this book, a wiser strategy would be to train the individual to independently use the supports (that is, prosthetic devices) that he or she needs to be successful both in and outside school.

CONTENT AREA: PLANNING/TIME MANAGEMENT

Managing Multistep Activities

Sample PLP for a ten-year-old student with ASD: According to informal observation and teacher report, student is able to perform simple one-step activities adequately; however, she presents with several organizational problems as a result of her EF deficits when tasks become more complex. This is particularly apparent in multistep activities where she will often bog down on a particular step and fail to complete the task. This difficulty affects her ability to independently complete assignments in a timely manner, if at all, in her inclusive fourth-grade classroom.

Goal/Objective Templates Based on PLP

Short-Term Objective 1:   Given a visual template depicting the steps in a multistep activity, student will complete a 3-step activity, within expected time frames, across 5 sets of activities at the 70% level, given direct verbal cues before each step.

Short-Term Objective 2:   Given a visual template, student will complete a 5-step activity, within expected time frames, across 5 sets of activities at the 80% level, given intermittent direct or indirect verbal cues.

Short-Term Objective 3:   Given a visual template, student will complete a 5-step activity, within expected time frames, across 7 sets of activities, given gestural cues.

Annual Goal: Given a visual template depicting the steps in a multistep activity, student will complete any multistep activity, within expected time frames, for all activities, independently.

Managing Long-Term Assignments

Sample PLP for a nine-year-old student with ADD and ED: According to clinical observation and teacher report, student is able to manage short-term assignments with an adequate degree of independence; however, when presented with a long-term project involving a number of steps, he has difficulty knowing where to begin and how to manage the various parts. He will often spend too much time on a small aspect of the project, and simply run out of time for the rest of it. These difficulties impact his ability to complete required long-term assignments in a timely manner and adversely affect his grades. They also provoke avoidance behavior.

Goal/Objective Templates Based on PLP

Short-Term Objective 1:   Given direct instruction in using a timeline template for completing long-term assignments, student will chain through each step in the time allotted, to complete 3 assignments, given direct verbal cues and ongoing monitoring.

Short-Term Objective 2:   Given a timeline template for completing long-term assignments, student will chain through each step in the time allotted, to complete 3 new, longer assignments, given indirect verbal cues and intermittent monitoring.

Short-Term Objective 3:   Given a timeline template for completing long-term assignments, student will chain through each step in the time allotted, to complete 3 new assignments, given intermittent, indirect monitoring (for example, "How are you doing with your project?").

Annual Goal: Given a timeline template for completing long-term assignments, student will chain through each step in the time allotted to complete academic assignments, given intermittent, indirect monitoring.

Explanatory Notes:

- In order to have a sufficient number of opportunities to work on this objective, we recommend fabricating "long-term" projects (for example, social studies/science assignments to be completed over a multiday or weeklong period).

- This objective could also be applied to planning future events, such as an in-class holiday party or other activity.

Basic Planning

Sample PLP for an eleven-year-old student with NLD: Student functions quite well in her inclusive classroom setting as long as she is told and shown exactly what to do. Her teacher reports, however, that she sometimes appears "at a loss" when directions are given. Her speech-language pathologist notes specific difficulty with time and ordinal concepts (for example, before/after; first/last). This difficulty causes student to become confused and impacts her ability to make time-based judgments and to follow directions in both her academic work and in group activities with peers.

Goal/Objective Templates Based on PLP

Short-Term Objective 1:   Given prior direct instruction and examples, and picture cards depicting the events in a story, student will demonstrate the ability to understand the language of planning (for example, first, next, last, before) by giving the picture card that corresponds to the question (for example, "What happened first?"), 7/10 questions for each of 2 time concepts (for example, first, last) across 5 stories, given direct verbal and gestural cues.

Short-Term Objective 2:   Given picture cards depicting the events in a story, student will demonstrate the ability to understand the language of planning by giving the picture card that corresponds to questions involving first/last time concepts, 8/10 questions, and before/next time concepts 7/10 questions across 5 stories, given indirect verbal or gestural cues.

Short-Term Objective 3:   Given picture cards depicting the events in a story, student will demonstrate the ability to understand the language of planning by giving the picture card that corresponds to questions involving all 4 time concepts, 8/10 questions for each, across 10 different stories, given expectant waiting.

Annual Goal: Student will demonstrate the ability to understand *first, next, last*, and *before* by answering questions and carrying out directives incorporating them, 80% of the time across stories and activities, independently.

CONTENT AREA: WORKING MEMORY

Holding Information "Online"

Sample PLP for a twelve-year-old student with ADD: Student is able to comprehend math concepts at an age-appropriate level; however, he has significant difficulty with math word problems, owing to difficulties keeping aspects of the problem "online" (that is, in working memory) while dealing with others. As a result of this problem, student has difficulty completing assignments and meeting grade-level expectations in math.

Goal/Objective Templates Based on PLP

Short-Term Objective 1:   Given direct instruction in the use of a math problem-solving template, student will fill in the required information from the word problem, and select from a choice of 3, the correct mathematical operation to use in solving the problem, 7/10 problems, with direct verbal cues and ongoing monitoring.

Short-Term Objective 2:   Given a math problem-solving template, student will fill in the required information from the word problem and independently determine the correct mathematical operation to use in solving the problem, 8/10 problems, with indirect verbal cues and intermittent monitoring.

Short-Term Objective 3:   Given a math problem-solving template, student will fill in the required information from the word problem, determine the correct mathematical operation to use, and solve the problem, 8/10 problems, with gestural cues as needed.

Annual Goal: Given a math problem-solving template, student will use the correct mathematical procedure to solve word problems with 80% accuracy, independently.

Sustaining Attention

Sample PLP for an eight-year-old student with ADHD: Student's performance on the weekly 50-item knowledge of math facts assessment indicates that while her knowledge of math facts is at grade level, she makes careless errors that reflect her difficulty with sustaining attention to task. As a result, she misses some problems entirely and performs incorrect mathematical operations on others because she fails to attend to the math operation sign changes. This difficulty negatively impacts her math test scores and causes her to be resistant to math work.

Goal/Objective Templates Based on PLP

Short-Term Objective 1:   Given a checklist reminding student to cover items row by row, look at the math operation sign, and check her answers, student will complete math tests with a maximum of 10 operation/omission errors per 50-item test, given direct verbal reminders to use the checklist and ongoing monitoring.

Short-Term Objective 2:   Given a 3-item checklist, student will complete weekly math tests with a maximum of 5 operation/omission errors per 50-item test, given no more than 3 indirect verbal reminders to use checklist and intermittent monitoring.

Short-Term Objective 3:   Given a 3-item check list, student will complete math tests with a maximum of 2 operation/omission errors per 50-item test, given no more than 2 gestural cues to use checklist and decreased intermittent monitoring.

Annual Goal: Student will independently use a checklist to complete math tests with a maximum of 1 operation/omission error per 50-item test.

GENERAL TEACHING TIPS AND STRATEGIES FOR EXECUTIVE FUNCTION SKILLS

1. Visual supports should be considered executive function "props." We recommend their frequent use in all settings. The following list contains examples of some of the many ways these supports may be used in both the school and home environments:

   - To illustrate activity sequences

   - To serve as a template for multistep tasks

   - To represent events

   - To demarcate time

   - To delineate tasks and assignments

   - To serve as reminders

   - To concretize abstract concepts and choices (for example, a turn marker)

   - To cue desirable behavior and language

   - To stabilize information

   - To facilitate self-monitoring

   - To increase understanding

   - To aid working memory

   - And so much more

2. Use color-coded materials as organizational tools (blue file for English; yellow file for math), and use self-help strategies such as cue cards and sticky notes as reminders.

3. Pair language input with visual cues such as pictures or manual signs, as events and activities are occurring, to capture and channel attention and to aid information processing. This also helps students to make the appropriate connections that lead to the establishment of meaning.

4. Construct a thermometer out of oak tag to serve as a mood/anger monitoring tool (low temp—good; high temp—need to use self-help strategies).

5. Use the *Time Timer,* game, and egg timers, as well as other visual means of demarcating time as tools for self-monitoring and time management, because they enable the student to see when he has "a lot" or "a little" time left to complete a task or enjoy a break.

CHAPTER

15

CRITICAL THINKING: AN ESSENTIAL LIFE SKILL

"Thinking is skilled work. It is not true that we are naturally endowed with the ability to think clearly and logically—without learning how, or without practicing."

—*Alfred Mander*

The students discussed in this volume have great difficulty with critical thinking. The importance of higher-order thinking skills cannot be overstated as they constitute the essential life skills needed "to prepare [children] for further education, employment, and independent living" (Wright and Wright, 2006, p. 20) as specified in IDEA 2004.

Critical thinking skills include these

- Getting the main idea

- Interpreting

- Sequencing

- Determining relevance

- Making inferences

- Making predictions and extending information

- Drawing conclusions

- Problem solving

- Making decisions/choices

- Reasoning

- Analyzing and synthesizing information

- Comparing/contrasting

- Negotiating

- Evaluating

- And so many more

RATIONALE FOR INCLUDING SKILL CATEGORY

- Research demonstrates that individuals with ASD present with deficits in many aspects of critical thinking (Minshew, Goldstein, Taylor, and Siegel, 1994; Twachtman-Cullen, 2000b, 2000c).

- Children with ADD/ADHD may also present with impairments in aspects of critical thinking, secondary to their distractibility and inattention, working memory problems, and impulsivity. This is particularly true for critical thinking tasks that require sustained attention and persistence.

- Although there may not be an organic basis for deficits in critical thinking, students with some types of ED can present with specific impairments in problem solving and in other areas of critical thinking as a result of unusual thought fixation patterns.

- Because children with NLD learn primarily through verbal language, they miss a tremendous amount of information, because only 35 percent of information comes from the verbal component (Tanguay, 2001). This means that the remaining two-thirds of information comes via nonverbal cues such as tone of voice and body language. Hence students with NLD have difficulty determining how a classmate or a character in a book might feel based on nonverbal cues. In addition, students with NLD have difficulty with other aspects of critical thinking, particularly when nonverbal information is needed for sense-making.

- Competence in critical thinking skills is crucial to higher-level thinking and reasoning, and to independent functioning overall.

PRESENT LEVELS OF PERFORMANCE FOR CRITICAL THINKING SKILLS

The PLP for critical thinking skills should include

- A statement indicating the student's strengths in critical thinking, particularly as they relate to academic achievement and functional performance

- A statement about the student's weaknesses in specific areas of critical thinking, particularly as they relate to academic achievement, functional performance, and priority educational needs for the coming year

- A statement on how the student's disability in critical thinking affects his or her involvement and progress in the general curriculum (or for preschool children, in appropriate activities)

- The sources of the statements in the PLP (optional)

- Any additional information that can enable the PLP to fulfill its two important functions: (1) to serve as the basis for generating need-based individualized IEP goals and objectives; and (2) to serve as the standard by which to judge student performance and progress

CONTENT AREA: BASIC CRITICAL THINKING SKILLS

Sequencing

Sample PLP for a six-year-old student with NLD: According to her teacher, student is able to answer specific questions about daily activities or the events in a story, but has difficulty relating these things in an appropriate order. The speech-language pathologist states that the student also has significant difficulty putting picture sequences in order in language therapy. These difficulties lead to problems with following instructional sequences and retelling events and stories, and they affect her play interactions with her peers.

Goal/Objective Templates Based on PLP

Short-Term Objective 1: Given direct instruction and the first card in a 3-step sequence, student will put the remaining 2 cards of the sequence in the correct order and answer questions about each step for 8 activity sequences, at an 80% accuracy level, given direct verbal and gestural cueing.

Short-Term Objective 2: Given the first card in a 4-step sequence, student will correctly put the remaining 3 cards of the sequence in the correct order and tell about each step for 10 activity sequences, at an 80% accuracy level, given indirect verbal cueing.

Short-Term Objective 3:   Given the first card in a 5-step sequence, student will correctly put the remaining 5 cards of the sequence in the correct order and tell about each step of the sequence, for 10 activity sequences, at an 80% accuracy level, given gestural cues.

Annual Goal: Given a 5-step, out-of-order series of sequence cards, student will arrange the cards in the correct order as she tells about each step for 10 new sequences at the 80% accuracy level, independently.

Predicting

Sample PLP for a seven-year-old student with ASD: Student is able to answer questions about factual material and the here and now. She is also hyperlexic (that is, evidences advanced reading decoding skills in the presence of reading comprehension difficulty). According to informal assessment and teacher observation, student has difficulty predicting what might come next in stories. This sequencing difficulty affects student's ability to extend stories, handle multistep activities, and play guessing games with peers.

Goal/Objective Templates Based on PLP

Short-Term Objective 1:   Given direct instruction in sequencing activities, and 3 picture cards in a 4-card sequence, student will choose the appropriate fourth card from a group of 3 choices, for 8 sequences, at an 80% accuracy rate, given direct verbal cues.

Short-Term Objective 2:   Given 3 picture cards in a 4-card sequence, student will choose the appropriate fourth card from a group of 5 choices, for 12 sequences, at an 80% accuracy rate, given indirect verbal cues.

Short-Term Objective 3:   Given 3 picture cards in a 4-card sequence, student will verbally predict what will happen next without seeing the card for 10 new sequences at an 80% accuracy rate, given expectant waiting.

Annual Goal: Student will accurately predict what will happen next, when asked, across 10 short stories, at an 80% accuracy level, independently.

Sample PLP for a twelve-year-old student with ED: According to performance on the *Test of Problem Solving (TOPS)*, student has difficulty in the area of predicting. This difficulty not only impedes his academic performance, particularly in English class, but also his relationship with peers. As for the latter, student often says or does inappropriate things that upset his peers and then is surprised by their negative reactions. His inability to predict the consequences of his actions causes him to blame his peers and to complain that they don't like him. As a result, student has missed classes and has had episodes in which he refuses to go to school.

Goal/Objective Templates Based on PLP

Short-Term Objective 1:   Given prior direct instruction and examples, and a setting event in a story scenario depicting a familiar social-conflict situation, student will predict how a particular character in the story will react, and state the reason for his answer, for 6/10 scenarios, given direct verbal cues and expanded input as needed.

Short-Term Objective 2:   Given a setting event in a story scenario depicting a familiar social-conflict situation, student will predict how a particular character in the story will react, and state the reason for his answer for 8/10 scenarios, given indirect verbal cues.

Short-Term Objective 3:   Given 10 role-play incomplete scripts, each involving a social conflict between 2 characters, student will select 1 card from a 3-card set that predicts the ending prior to viewing the videotaped role-play, 8/10 opportunities, given indirect verbal cues as needed.

Annual Goal: Given an incomplete script involving a social conflict between 2 characters, student will independently predict the possible ending prior to viewing the videotaped role-play, 8/10 opportunities, independently.

Determining Feelings

Sample PLP for an eight-year-old student with NLD: Student demonstrates significant difficulty determining how characters in stories feel both in standardized testing and in classroom reading activities. This affects her ability to comprehend narratives and to write book reports. In addition, student also demonstrates an inability to recognize the displeasure of her classmates when she says or does something that offends them, even though their body language "says it all," according to her teacher.

Goal/Objective Templates Based on PLP

Short-Term Objective 1:   Given direct instruction/demonstration regarding facial expressions and 10 short stories in which the main characters depict emotions that flow from the story line (for example, angry, sad, happy, worried, bored), student will choose the emotional response that accurately reflects the character's facial expression from a group of three cards, 8/10 opportunities, given direct verbal cues.

Short-Term Objective 2: Given 10 different short stories in which the main characters depict emotions that flow from the storyline, student will name the emotion that accurately reflects the character's facial expression, 8/10 opportunities, given indirect verbal cues.

Short-Term Objective 3: Given 10 videotaped role-plays in which the main characters act out emotions that fit the context, student will name the emotion that accurately reflects the character's facial expression and body language, 8/10 opportunities, given expectant waiting.

Annual Goal: Student will demonstrate understanding of specific emotions by responding accurately to questions, in class, regarding the feelings of characters in stories, 8/10 opportunities, independently.

CONTENT AREA: INFERENCES

Making Concrete Inferences

Sample PLP for a fourteen-year-old student with ASD: According to formal assessment and teacher report, student is able to deal effectively with factual material, often scoring well above many of his peers on both standardized and teacher-made tests. His ability to make even simple inferences, however, lags far behind. This makes it difficult for student to deal with essay tests that require him to move beyond a factual level. Moreover, because of his problems with inferential material, he tends to take everything literally. These difficulties have caused some of his classmates to make fun of him, and have created significant problems for him in academic subjects that require inferential understanding.

Goal/Objective Templates Based on PLP

Short-Term Objective 1: Given direct teaching in inference-making/examples, and a series of 10 picture cards depicting a variety of common situations (for example, a boy with a bat staring at a broken window), student will infer what happened, 8/10 opportunities, given direct and indirect verbal cues.

Short-Term Objective 2: Given a series of 10 new and 10 previous picture cards depicting a variety of common situations, student will infer what happened, 8/10 opportunities, given indirect verbal cues as needed.

Short-Term Objective 3: Given 20 short story passages describing a series of events, student will infer how each story will end, 9/10 opportunities, given expectant waiting.

Annual Goal: Student will infer what happened in situations depicted in reading assignments by answering questions appropriately 9/10 opportunities, independently.

Making Abstract Inferences—Verbal

Sample PLP for a nine-year-old student with ED: Student performs in the impaired range on the Making Inferences section of the *Test of Problem Solving (TOPS)* and the Inference section of the *Comprehensive Assessment of Spoken Language (CASL),* with scores in other measured areas being age-appropriate. In class, she understands information that is directly stated, but has difficulty "reading between the lines" to fill in missing information. This difficulty negatively affects her performance on comprehension tests, as well as her ability to follow classroom routines and directions, solve problems, and respond appropriately in social situations.

Goal/Objective Templates Based on PLP

Short-Term Objective 1: Given prior direct instruction, when presented with a scenario in which information is missing (for example, short written narrative with implied information; sequence card story with beginning or middle step missing), student will identify the missing step/information from a multiple-choice format, 6/10 scenarios, given direct verbal cues and explanation as needed.

Short-Term Objective 2: When presented with a scenario in which information is missing, student will infer the missing information based on story/picture content, 7/10 scenarios, given indirect verbal cues.

Short-Term Objective 3: When presented with a scenario in which information is missing, student will infer the missing information based on story/picture content and give the reason for her inference, 8/10 scenarios, given expectant waiting.

Annual Goal: Student will make abstract inferences across all school subjects 8/10 opportunities, independently.

Sample PLP for a seven-year-old student with ADHD and NLD: Student does well in reading decoding and in tasks involving procedural knowledge. He has significant difficulty with many critical thinking skill areas, particularly where inferential understanding is required, often complaining that "it doesn't say that" when the teacher tells the students something about a character. This difficulty is negatively affecting student's grades in language arts and social studies, and interfering with some of his activities with peers on the playground.

Short-Term Objective 1:   Given direct verbal instruction in inference-making, and a series of 10 picture cards depicting a variety of common situations (for example, a girl looking at an empty glass on the floor), student will infer what happened, 8/10 opportunities, given direct and indirect verbal cues.

Short-Term Objective 2:   Given a series of 10 picture cards depicting a variety of common situations/events, student will infer a character's reaction to the outcome, 8/10 opportunities, given direct questions. (For example, "How will Dad react to the spilled milk?")

Short-Term Objective 3:   Given a series of 10 short stories, student will infer the reactions of characters to the events in the stories and state the reason for their reactions, 8/10 opportunities, given indirect questions as needed.

Annual Goal: Student will infer the reactions of characters to the events depicted in stories and textbook passages across language arts and social studies classes, 8/10 opportunities, given expectant time delay or indirect verbal cues as needed.

Making Abstract Inferences—Nonverbal

Sample PLP for an eleven-year-old student with NLD: According to performance on the *Social Language Development Test (SLDT)*, student presents with moderate to severe impairments in the ability to interpret nonverbal signals such as facial expressions and gestures. Core language, as assessed by the *Clinical Evaluation of Language Fundamentals (CELF)*, is age-appropriate. Student's difficulty with reading nonverbal cues impairs her social relationships with both children and adults, as she fails to read their behavioral cues. As a result, student is subjected to frequent reprimands by her teacher and is a target for bullying. These difficulties cause her to miss lessons in class and negatively affect her ability to focus, leading to poor academic performance.

Goal/Objective Templates Based on PLP

Short-Term Objective 1:   Given prior instruction in the meaning of various facial expressions and nonverbal signals in the context of 5 familiar stories and 5 videotaped role-play sequences, student will identify the character's/person's emotion and the reason for it, 80% of the time for each context, given direct verbal and manual sign cues.

Short-Term Objective 2: Given 5 unfamiliar (new) stories and 5 new video-taped role-play sequences, student will identify the character's/person's emotion and the reason for it, 80% of the time for each context, given indirect verbal or gestural cues.

Short-Term Objective 3: Given 5 unfamiliar (new) stories and 5 scripts from previous role-play sequences, student will identify the character's/person's emotion and the reason for it in the story, and act out appropriate emotional reactions in the role-plays, 90% of the time for each context, given gestural cues.

Annual Goal: Student will both identify emotions and state the reasons for them in story characters, and will respond appropriately to nonverbal emotional signals in real-life situations with minimal indirect verbal and gestural cueing.

CONTENT AREA: PROBLEM SOLVING

Sample PLP for a sixteen-year-old student with moderate autism: When given visual supports, and when activities proceed as expected, student is able to complete assignments in his classroom and work settings in a timely manner. His teacher and vocational supervisor report, however, that he becomes confused and unable to complete his work when even minor problems interrupt his activities. Formal testing via the *Test of Problem Solving—Adolescent* also indicates difficulty in this area. These problems negatively affect his ability to function independently in both classroom and work-related settings.

Goal/Objective Templates Based on PLP

Short-Term Objective 1: Given direct instruction/demonstration in the use of a problem-solving template, and a series of 5 problem scenarios, student will choose an appropriate solution from 2 options presented, 4/5 opportunities, given direct coaching.

Short-Term Objective 2: Given a problem-solving template, and a series of 10 new problem scenarios, student will choose an appropriate solution from 3 options presented, 4/5 opportunities, with indirect coaching.

Short-Term Objective 3: Given a problem-solving template, and a series of 10 new problem scenarios, student will apply a problem-solving strategy appropriate to the situation in structured role-plays with 2 to 3 peers, 4/5 opportunities, given indirect coaching.

Annual Goal: Student will use a problem-solving template to apply an appropriate problem-solving strategy in contrived classroom situations, 4/5 opportunities, given expectant waiting or manual sign cues as needed.

Sample PLP for a fourteen-year-old student with ED: Although he is capable of completing class work at grade level, student becomes very agitated when unexpected problems occur in class. His behavior not only prevents him from completing his school work but is also disruptive to his classmates, and poses a safety concern during unstructured times (such as lunch and study hall). Testing with the *Test of Problem Solving—Adolescent* indicates significant impairments in the ability to identify problems and suggest solutions.

Goal/Objective Templates Based on PLP

Short-Term Objective 1: Given direct instruction, a problem-solving 4-item solution card, and 10 problem scenarios presented in a calm, quiet setting, student will identify the problem from 4 possible choices and select an appropriate solution for it, at an 80% accuracy level for each, given direct verbal cueing.

Short-Term Objective 2: Given a problem-solving 4-item solution card and 10 problem scenarios presented in a calm, quiet setting, student will independently identify the problem and select an appropriate solution for it, at an 80% accuracy level for each, given expectant waiting or indirect verbal cueing as needed.

Short-Term Objective 3: Given a problem-solving 4-item solution card, student will select and apply problem-solving strategies to actual situations in 2 teacher-contrived problem scenarios in the classroom and 1 unstructured activity (for example, the lunchroom), 80% of the time, given indirect verbal or manual sign cues to use his solution card.

Annual Goal: Given a portable problem-solving solution card, student will independently select and apply solutions to actual problem situations when they occur, across environments and activities for 80% of problems encountered with minimal indirect verbal or manual sign cues to use his solution card.

Explanatory Note: The portable, pocket-sized card with a list of 4 optional solutions that the student will carry with him is considered an accommodation.

CONTENT AREA: ANALYZING AND SYNTHESIZING INFORMATION

Sample PLP for an eight-year-old student with ASD: During her speech therapy sessions, student is able to name attributes of an object when asked, but she is not able to determine commonalities or differences between object pairs. These difficulties negatively affect her ability to perform comparative tasks as required by her second-grade science curriculum.

Goal/Objective Templates Based on PLP

Short-Term Objective 1:   Given demonstration and direct instruction, student will sort objects into same/different categories, 9/10 opportunities.

Short-Term Objective 2:   Given a pair of objects that are similar to and different from each other based on known concepts, and an attribute template (for example, color, size, shape), student will state 1–2 similarities and 1–2 differences between object pairs for 9/10 pairs, given direct verbal cues as needed.

Short-Term Objective 3:   Given a pair of objects that are similar to and different from each other based on known concepts, student will compare objects by stating 2 ways in which they are similar to and 2 ways in which they are different from one another for 9/10 object pairs, given indirect verbal cues.

Annual Goal: Student will compare and contrast objects by stating 2–3 ways in which they are similar to and different from one another, 8/10 opportunities, independently.

CONTENT AREA: DRAWING CONCLUSIONS

Sample PLP for a fifteen-year-old student with ADD: As part of his history curriculum, student is asked to write essays that require him to compare and contrast historical events, and then draw conclusions about them. Although he is able to answer specific questions about events if his teacher lists the advantages and disadvantages in chart form, he is unable to analyze and synthesize this information in order to draw conclusions. This difficulty is apparent in both class discussions and in his essays. As a result of these problems, he is failing his American history class.

Short-Term Objective 1: Given a 5-item teacher-generated list of happenings for each of 4 historical events, student will select 2 each that are advantageous/disadvantageous and state the reason for each choice, at an 80% level of accuracy for each circumstance, given direct verbal cueing.

Short-Term Objective 2:   Given a 5-item teacher-generated list of happenings for each of 4 historical events, student will select 3 advantages/disadvantages and state the reason for each choice, at an 80% level of accuracy for each circumstance, given indirect verbal cueing.

Short-Term Objective 3:   Given 4 sets of historical events, student will fill in information on a template designed for comparing, contrasting, and drawing conclusions between each set of events at an 80% level of accuracy for each element, given indirect verbal cueing.

Annual Goal: Student will independently employ a template to compare, contrast, and draw conclusions about events covered in his history curriculum at an 80% level of accuracy, with minimal indirect verbal cueing.

CONTENT AREA: DETERMINING RELEVANCE

Sample PLP for a thirteen-year-old student with NLD: When reading stories or textbooks student is able to recall some details, but these are not always the details that are most relevant to the plot of the story or lesson in the text. Student's reading comprehension for details is age-appropriate, but she currently makes little distinction between information that is relevant and information that is irrelevant. As a result, she has difficulty comprehending the overall plot of a story or getting the correct information from lessons in a text. This negatively affects both her performance on tests and her grades.

Goal/Objective Templates Based on PLP

Short-Term Objective 1:   Given direct instruction and a 6-item multiple-choice format containing both relevant and irrelevant details for 10 stories or textbook passages, student will select 2 relevant details corresponding to the story or textbook passage, across 10 stories or passages, 9/10 opportunities, given direct verbal cueing.

Short-Term Objective 2:   Given a 6-item multiple-choice format containing both relevant and irrelevant details for 10 stories or textbook passages, student will select 3 relevant details corresponding to the story or textbook passage, across 5 new stories or passages, given indirect verbal cueing.

Short-Term Objective 3:   Given cloze sentences, student will generate a minimum of 3 relevant details of a story/textbook passage across 10 previous and 5 new stories/passages, 9/10 opportunities, given expectant waiting and indirect verbal cues as needed.

Annual Goal: Student will give a minimum of 3 relevant details of a story or textbook passage across all appropriate academic subjects with only occasional indirect verbal or gestural cues.

GENERAL TEACHING TIPS AND STRATEGIES FOR CRITICAL THINKING SKILLS

1. Stage problems in the classroom, verbally go through the steps to take to solve the problem, and then solve it. For example: "Hmmm, I can't find my pencil. Let's see, could it be on the desk? No, I had it when I was helping Jamie in the back of the classroom. I think I'll look there. Great! Here it is."

2. For preschool children, use cause-effect toys to illustrate causal relationships that the child can directly control through his or her own actions.

3. Use sequence cards and children's literature to promote the development of critical thinking skills. For example, to work on prediction using a book with a naturally occurring prediction format, such as *If You Give a Mouse a Cookie*, ask the question posed in the title, "If you give a mouse a cookie, what will he ask for next?" Continue to ask the question for each item requested, for a veritable powerhouse of prediction opportunities! This activity can even be used with nonverbal children by having them select—from a group of objects representing the events in the story—the item that "predicts" what will happen next.

4. Make the connections for the student in situations requiring inferential reasoning that he or she might not be able to make independently. For example, in the story of *Goldilocks and the Three Bears,* neurotypical preschool children readily infer that if Goldilocks is eating from the little bowl, then the bowl must belong to Baby Bear. To ensure that children with ASD make the appropriate connection, we recommend supplying it for them. (For example, "That must be Baby Bear's bowl, because it's so little.")

5. Allow students to *appropriately* negotiate for such things as more computer time or a special privilege. Remember, even very young children learn how negotiate for a cookie when Mom says no. To wit: "Please may I have a cookie?" "Pretty please?!"

EPILOGUE

A great deal has changed since 2002 when we wrote *How Well Does Your IEP Measure Up?* Change, of course, is not always positive; neither is progress—in the sense of advancement toward the goal—if one is on the wrong road.

First things first! What is the goal—or in keeping with the metaphor—the destination of special education? In the most basic sense, it is to provide students with disabilities with a free appropriate public education (FAPE) that is individualized to their needs. The terms *appropriate* and *individualized* are critical. Although the standard of *appropriateness* has never been defined, we can all agree that the term is relative—that it takes into account the individual needs of each student. Hence, what is appropriate for one student may not be appropriate—or may even be inappropriate—for another. We can also agree that *individualization*—building educational goals and objectives around the specific needs of the student—is at the heart of the IEP.

Fast-forward to the Individuals with Disabilities Education Improvement Act of 2004 (IDEA 2004): clearly, the reauthorized act raises the bar on what constitutes FAPE. The good news is that there is a recognition of and new emphasis on the importance of having high expectations for students with disabilities and on highly qualified educators. Likewise, there is greater accountability in the call for research-based instruction and improved outcomes for students. Had IDEA 2004 stayed on its winding, sometimes rocky road to FAPE armed with the clout these welcome new additions afford, I would be writing a very different epilogue to this book. Sadly, that is not the case. Unfortunately, IDEA 2004 veered off-course and took a fork in the road marked *No Child Left Behind*. Although few may be willing to acknowledge it, it is clear to me that we are on a different road and that our destination has changed. No longer, it

179

seems, is the goal that of education that is appropriate and individualized to the needs of each specific student, for NCLB has conferred a different standard.

Given its alignment with NCLB, the new and "improved" IDEA has created an avalanche of unintended consequences for students with special needs. For one thing, *appropriateness* is no longer relative—that is, based on the needs of the student—but rather tied to the "challenging expectations that have been established for *all* children" [emphasis supplied] (Steedman, Summer 2005). Nowhere is this more obvious than in the case of students with the most significant challenges, for IDEA 2004 mandates that the alternate assessments they take be "aligned with the State's challenging academic content standards and challenging student academic achievement standards" (20 U.S.C. 1412[a][16][C][ii][l]). So, for example, what is appropriate for nondisabled students—*cognitively capable of mastering challenging academic content and meeting challenging achievement goals*—has somehow become the standard bearer for even the most significantly challenged students. This mandate has local education authorities (LEAs) bending over backwards to come up with watered-down, irrelevant, and often ridiculous test questions in order to mirror academic content for nondisabled peers—for example, having the student identify the place where the wall meets the floor as evidence of his or her understanding of what a right angle is. So much for appropriateness!

Another unintended consequence of IDEA 2004 is that it requires states to "establish performance goals for children with disabilities that are the *same* [emphasis supplied] as the state's definition of adequate yearly progress under NCLB" (Steedman, Summer 2005). Thus, if students with disabilities who lag significantly behind their nondisabled peers are to narrow the academic achievement gap, they must make more than a year's worth of progress in a single academic year (Steedman, Summer 2005). That would seem to put IDEA 2004 in service to NCLB, even as it steamrolls over students with special needs by holding them to arbitrary and inappropriate standards. So much for individualization!

As the foregoing clearly indicates, there is also a much greater emphasis on academics in IDEA 2004 that is yet another reflection of NCLB. This, however, ignores a basic and crucial reality—that it is not necessarily a lack of academic progress that keeps students with ASD, NLD, ADD/ADHD, S/LI, or ED from leading successful and productive lives. Indeed, students with these conditions can and often do meet challenging academic standards but still fail to lead "productive and independent lives" (the standard set forth in IDEA 2004). The reason for this is that the self-same difficulties they manifest—as for example, in social cognition, executive function, communication, and so forth—are the very skills needed to lead successful lives.

Add to all of this the experimentation with three-year IEPs in some states, and the form-over-substance elimination of short-term objectives and benchmarks for the majority of students with special needs, as a sop for beleaguered school personnel eager to avoid paperwork, and one has to wonder exactly whose best interests Congress had in mind with IDEA 2004.

The IEP from A to Z is our attempt, in the words of C. S. Lewis, at "doing an about-turn and walking back to the right road," for in this book we do address those areas of functioning that are eminently tied to leading productive and independent lives. We also urge IEP teams to honor the "good fit" over the "quick fix" when it comes to creating IEPs for students with special needs. That will mean writing short-term objectives or benchmarks for *all* students, even though it means more paperwork. Think of it this way: to have only an annual goal, without a plan for reaching it—the short-term objectives or benchmarks— is like trying to reach an unknown destination without a set of directions or a map.

As we end our "journey of a thousand miles" we do so knowing that we are on the right road, for as we stated in the Introduction, we have operated from the perspective of what is in the best educational interests of the student. It is our fondest wish that *The IEP from A to Z* will enable IEP teams to fulfill their obligation to students by helping them build education programs that are appropriate and individualized to the needs of those students so that they may lead successful, productive, and independent lives.

Diane Twachtman-Cullen, Ph.D., CCC-SLP

APPENDIX

TIPS FOR TEACHING SKILL DEVELOPMENT AND GENERALIZATION

In the days when most students with special needs were assigned to special education classrooms, and speech-language pathologists (SLPs) had not yet abandoned their therapy rooms, finding a time and a place for skill development was a lot easier. Today, with the emphasis on inclusion and the collaborative consultation model, the regular education classroom has become a noisy, bustling, complex environment that does not easily afford quiet opportunities for the repetition and practice that many students need to acquire skills. So, what's an educator or therapist to do?

As the reader will note, many of the deficit areas addressed in this book can best be addressed through role-plays in which students can "try out" skills in a contrived, supportive, and low-key environment before taking them on the road, so to speak, and actually applying them in the classroom and elsewhere. And because there is no substitute for a quiet therapy room for this purpose, SLPs and other therapists are encouraged to use their therapy rooms as learning labs for initial skill development.

For those skills that can be addressed and monitored in the general education setting—and for generalization work on skills that were addressed in more restrictive settings—we suggest the following teaching formats for working on goals and objectives:

- Day-to-day school activities and classroom routines provide excellent vehicles for working on skills. For example, morning circle, centers, and snack time provide rich opportunities for younger children to practice important skills. Likewise, morning meetings, leisure activities, and work stations work well for older students.

- Field trips and community-based and vocational activities can also be used for skill development.

- Songs, nursery rhymes, and rhythmic activities are great for working on social interaction, play, and language among preschoolers.

- Planning, time management, and organizational skills may be addressed through art projects, group activities, and long-term assignments for both younger and older students, but don't forget the visual supports.

- Recess can be a great "generalization lab" for many skills, not to mention an ideal environment for learning to play and get along with others. The key here is to work in organized activities (like games with rules) in which there are specific roles, structure, and facilitation and monitoring by adults.

- Interactive story routines in preschool are an ideal way to work on language, vocabulary, and critical thinking skills such as predicting, inferring, and sequencing. Reading activities also provide great opportunities for older students to work on the elements of story grammar and higher-order critical thinking such as getting the main idea and problem solving.

- "Lunch-bunch" groups are great for generalizing social skills or for working on activities such as engaging in small talk—a task that looms large for many students with ASD, NLD, and ED.

- Many skills—for example, narrative development—can be directly addressed in academic activities in the classroom setting.

- "Specials," such as physical education and music, can provide opportunities for practice and skill generalization, particularly if a teaching assistant is assigned to one or more students to monitor student performance.

- The resource room is a great setting for working on lots of different skills for students.

- Extended environments, such as the home, afterschool clubs, and extracurricular activities, are particularly important for promoting the generalization of skills. Needless to say, a great deal of planning is required.

Generating meaningful and measurable annual goals and short-term objectives is a very important first step in addressing skill development in children with special needs. But it is only the *first* step. If students are to acquire and *use* skills, there must be direct and ongoing attention to working on those goals and objectives across settings, people, and activities. This takes commitment, planning, and teamwork on the part of educators and therapists alike. The list of teaching formats shown here is not exhaustive by any means. However, we hope it will encourage school personnel to seek out additional opportunities for skill development, whether by taking advantage of break time to play a critical thinking skills game or sending the student to the office on a contrived mission to practice requesting.

APPENDIX

HELPFUL TEACHING RESOURCES

The following teaching resources, listed alphabetically by title, are a sampling of those that we feel will provide high-quality information and guidance on meeting IEP goals and objectives for students with ADD/ADHD, ASD, NLD, ED, and S/LI. With the exception of the ASD-specific and miscellaneous titles listed at the end, the teaching resources are categorized according to specific skill areas as a convenience to the reader, and may be used across a wide range of disabilities and functioning levels.

In addition, it should be noted that the Library of Speech Pathology Book Club (717–918–4120) is an excellent repository for difficult-to-find resources on communication, language, and critical thinking.

COMMUNICATION AND LANGUAGE DEVELOPMENT

Concept Acquisition Procedures for Preschoolers (CAPP): Levels 1, 2, & 3. C. Weiner. Youngtown, AZ: ECL Publications.
Conceptbuilding: Developing Meaning through Narratives and Discussion. P. Reichardt. Eau Claire, WI: Thinking Publications.
Dyspraxia: A Guide for Teachers and Parents. K. Ripley, B. Daines, and J. Barrett. London: David Fulton Publishers.
Early Communication Skills. C. Lynch and J. Kidd. Oxfordshire, United Kingdom: Winslow Press Ltd.

Excell: Experiences in Context for Early Language Learning. C. B. Raack. Tuscon, AZ: Communication Skill Builders.

Figurative Language: A Comprehensive Program. K. A. Gorman-Gard. Eau Claire, WI: Thinking Publications.

Interactive Language Skills. J. G. DeGaetano. Wrightsville Beach, NC: Great Ideas for Teaching.

It Takes Two to Talk: A Practical Guide for Parents of Children with Language Delays. J. Pepper and E. Weitzman. Toronto, Ontario, Canada: The Hanen Centre.

Listening, Understanding, Remembering, Verbalizing! J. G. DeGaetano. Wrightsville Beach, NC: Great Ideas for Teaching, Inc.

Shared Storybook Reading. H. K. Ezell and L. M. Justice. Baltimore: Paul H. Brookes Publishing Co.

CRITICAL THINKING SKILLS DEVELOPMENT

Activities for Mastering Inferences. J. G. DeGaetano. Wrightsville Beach, NC: Great Ideas for Teaching.

Critical Thinking Handbook: K–3rd Grades, A Guide for Remodeling Lesson Plans in Language Arts, Social Studies, and Science. R. W. Paul, A.J.A. Brinker, and D. Weil. Dillon Beach, CA: Foundation for Critical Thinking.

Critical Thinking Handbook: High School: A Guide for Redesigning Instruction. R. W. Paul, D. Martin, and K. Adamson. Dillon Beach, CA: Foundation for Critical Thinking.

Developing Logical Reasoning. J. G. DeGaetano. Wrightsville Beach, NC: Great Ideas for Teaching.

Introducing Inference. M. M. Toomey. Marblehead, MA: Circuit Publications. (Direct sales only.)

Preschool First Sequence Pictures (Sets 1 & 2). Marblehead, MA: Circuit Publications. (Direct sales only.)

Problem-Solving Activities. J. G. DeGaetano. Wrightsville Beach, NC: Great Ideas for Teaching.

Problem-Solving Workbook. T. Zimmerman. King of Prussia, PA: Center for Applied Psychology.

Talk About Planning. M. M. Toomey. Marblehead, MA: Circuit Publications. (Direct sales only.)

EXECUTIVE FUNCTION SKILLS DEVELOPMENT

ADHD Book of Lists: A Practical Guide for Helping Children and Teens with Attention Deficit Disorders. S. F. Rief. San Francisco: Jossey-Bass.

Attention-Deficit Hyperactivity Disorder: A Clinical Workbook, Third Edition. R. A. Barkley and K. R. Murphy. New York: Guilford Press.

Disorganized Children: A Guide for Parents and Professionals. S. M. Stein and U. Chowdhury. London and Philadelphia: Jessica Kingsley Publishers.

Executive Skills in Children and Adolescents, Second Edition: A Practical Guide to Assessment and Intervention. P. Dawson and R. Guare. New York: Guilford Press.

Help for the Struggling Student: Ready-to-Use Strategies and Lessons to Build Attention, Memory, and Organizational Skills. M. Gold. San Francisco: Jossey-Bass.

How to Reach and Teach Children with ADD/ADHD: Practical Techniques, Strategies, and Interventions, 2nd Edition. S. F. Rief. San Francisco: Jossey-Bass.

Revealing Minds: Assessing to Understand and Support Struggling Learners. C. Pohlman. San Francisco: Jossey-Bass.

Smart but Scattered: The Revolutionary "Executive Skills" Approach to Helping Kids Reach Their Potential. P. Dawson and R. Guare. New York: Guilford Press.

Socially ADDept: A Manual for Parents of Children with ADHD and/or Learning Disabilities. J. Z. Giler. San Francisco: Jossey-Bass.

Strategies for Teaching Adolescents with ADHD: Effective Classroom Techniques Across the Content Areas, Grades 6–12. S. L. DeRuvo. San Francisco: Jossey-Bass.

NARRATIVE SKILLS DEVELOPMENT

Expanding and Combining Sentences. M. M. Toomey. Marblehead, MA: Circuit Publications. (Direct sales only.)

Explaining. M. M. Toomey. Marblehead, MA: Circuit Publications. (Direct sales only.)

Narrative Toolbox: Blueprints for Storybuilding. P. Hudson-Nechkash. Eau Claire, WI: Thinking Publications.

Preschool First Stories. M. M. Toomey. Marblehead, MA: Circuit Publications. (Direct sales only.)

Telling a Story. M. M. Toomey. Marblehead, MA: Circuit Publications (Direct sales only.)

Themestorming. J. Becker, K. Reid, P. Steinhaus, and P. Wieck. Beltsville, MD: Gryphon House.

NONVERBAL LEARNING SKILLS DEVELOPMENT

Helping Children with Nonverbal Learning Disabilities to Flourish: A Guide for Parents and Professionals. M. Martin. London and Philadelphia: Jessica Kingsley Publishers.

Helping the Child Who Doesn't Fit In. S. Nowicki, Jr., and M. P. Duke. Atlanta: Peachtree Publishers.

Nonverbal Learning Disabilities at Home: A Parent's Guide. P. B. Tanguay. London and Philadelphia: Jessica Kingsley Publishers.

Nonverbal Learning Disabilities at School: Educating Students with NLD, Asperger Syndrome, and Related Conditions. P. B. Tanguay. London and Philadelphia: Jessica Kingsley Publishers.

Source for Nonverbal Learning Disorders. S. Thompson. East Moline, IL: LinguiSystems.

Teaching Your Child the Language of Social Success. M. Duke, S. Nowicki, and E. Martin. Atlanta: Peachtree Press.

PLAY SKILLS DEVELOPMENT

Peer Play and the Autism Spectrum: The Art of Guiding Children's Socialization and Imagination. P. J. Wolfberg. Shawnee Mission, KS: Autism Asperger Publishing Co.

Play and Imagination in Children with Autism. P. J. Wolfberg. New York: Teachers College Press.

Transdisciplinary Play-Based Assessment, Second Edition (spiral-bound). Toni Linder. Baltimore: Paul H. Brookes Publishing Co.

Transdisciplinary Play-Based Intervention, Second Edition (spiral-bound). Toni Linder. Baltimore: Paul H. Brookes Publishing.

SOCIAL-EMOTIONAL SKILLS DEVELOPMENT AND ANGER MANAGEMENT

Adolescent Problems, Second Edition. D. Nicolson and H. Ayers. London: David Fulton Publishers.

Emotional and Behavioral Problems of Young Children: Effective Interventions in the Preschool and Kindergarten Years. G. G. Peacock. New York: Guilford Press.

Expressing Emotion: Myths, Realities, and Therapeutic Strategies. E. Kennedy-Moore and J. C. Watson. New York: Guilford Press.

Power of Guidance: Teaching Social-Emotional Skills in Early Childhood Classrooms. D. Gartrell. Belmont, CA: Wadsworth.

131 Creative Strategies for Reaching Children with Anger Problems (Grades 1–5). Tom Carr. Champaign, IL: Research Press.

141 Creative Strategies for Reaching Adolescents with Anger Problems (Grades 6–12). Tom Carr. Champaign, IL: Research Press.

SOCIAL SKILLS DEVELOPMENT

More Social Skills Stories: Very Personal Picture Stories for Readers and Nonreaders K–12. A. M. Johnson. Solana Beach, CA: Mayer-Johnson Co.

New Social Story Book (revised and expanded 10th anniversary edition). C. Gray. Arlington, TX: Future Horizons.

Social Behavior Mapping: Connecting Behavior, Emotions and Consequences Across the Day. M. G. Winner. San Jose, CA: Think Social Publishing.

Social Skills Activities for Special Children. D. Mannix. West Nyack, NY: Center for Applied Research in Education.

Social Skills Picture Book: Teaching Play, Emotion, and Communication to Children with Autism. Jed Baker. Arlington, TX: Future Horizons.

Social Skills Stories: Functional Picture Stories for Readers and Nonreaders K–12. A. M. Johnson and J. L. Susnik. Solana Beach, CA: Mayer-Johnson Co.

Social Skill Strategies: A Social-Emotional Curriculum for Adolescents (Book A). N. Gajewski, P. Hirn, and P. Mayo. Eau Claire, WI: Thinking Publications.

Social Skills Training. J. E. Baker, Ph.D. Shawnee Mission, KS: Autism Asperger Publishing.

Socially Curious and Curiously Social. M. G. Winner. San Jose, CA: Think Social Publishing.

THEORY OF MIND INTERVENTION

Teaching Children with Autism to Mind-Read: A Practical Guide. P. Howlin, S. Baron-Cohen, and J. Hadwin. Hoboken, NJ: Wiley.
Theory of Mind: How Children Understand Others' Thoughts and Feelings. M. J. Doherty. London: Psychology Press.

BEHAVIOR INTERVENTION

Challenging Behavior in Young Children: Understanding, Preventing, and Responding Effectively, Second Edition. B. Kaiser and J. Rasminsky. Boston: Allyn & Bacon.
Solving Behavior Problems in Autism. L. Hodgdon. Troy, MI: Quirk Roberts.

AUTISM- AND ASPERGER SYNDROME–SPECIFIC GENERAL INFORMATION RESOURCES

Asperger Syndrome: A Practical Guide for Teachers. V. Cumine, J. Leach, and G. Stevenson. London: David Fulton Publishers.
Complete Guide to Asperger Syndrome. Tony Attwood. London and Philadelphia: Jessica Kingsley Publishers.
Learners on the Autism Spectrum: Preparing Highly Qualified Educators. K. D. Buron and P. Wolfberg. Shawnee Mission, KS: Autism Asperger Publishing.
Source for Intervention in Autism Spectrum Disorders. Phyllis Kupperman. East Moline, IL: LinguiSystems.
Stress and Coping in Autism. M. G. Baron, J. Groden, G, Groden, and L. P. Lipsitt, editors. New York: Oxford University Press.
Teaching Children with Autism: Strategies to Enhance Communication and Socialization. Kathleen Ann Quill, editor. Delmar.

MISCELLANEOUS RESOURCES FOR MULTIPLE DISABILITY CATEGORIES

How to Be a Para Pro: A Comprehensive Training Manual for Paraprofessionals. D. Twachtman-Cullen. Higganum, CT: Starfish Specialty Press, LLC.
Incredible 5-Point Scale. K. D. Buron. Shawnee Mission, KS: Autism Asperger Publishing.
Relaxation: A Comprehensive Manual for Adults, Children, and Children with Special Needs (spiral bound). J. R. Cautela and J. Groden. Champaign, IL: Research Press.
Time Timer. A visual tool for telling time developed by J. Rogers. To order call 877-771-8463 or log onto www.timetimer.com.
Visual Strategies for Improving Communication. L. Hodgdon. Troy, MI: Quirk Roberts.

REFERENCES

Barkley, R. A. (2006). *Attention-deficit hyperactivity disorder: A handbook for diagnosis and treatment (3rd ed.)*. New York: Guilford Press

Baron-Cohen, S., Tager-Flusberg, H., & Cohen, D. J. (1993). *Understanding other minds: Perspectives from autism*. Oxford, England: Oxford University Press.

Bateman, B. D., & Herr, C. M. (2006). *Writing measurable IEP goals and objectives*. Verona, WI: Attainment Company.

Berkell, D. E. (1992). Instructional planning: Goals and practice. In D. E. Berkell (ed.), *Autism: Identification, education, and treatment* (pp. 89–105). Hillsdale, NJ: Erlbaum.

Board of Education v. Rowley, 458 U.S. 176 (1982).

Bodrova, E., & Leong, D. J. (2007). *Tools of the mind: The Vygotskian approach to early childhood education* (2nd ed.). Upper Saddle River, NJ: Pearson Education.

Carr, E. G., & Kologinsky, E. (1983). Acquisition of sign language by autistic children II: Spontaneity and generalization effects. *Journal of Applied Behavior Analysis*, *16*, 297–314.

Cayne, B. (1989). *The new Lexicon Webster's dictionary of the English language* (encyclopedic ed.). New York: Lexicon Publications.

Costello, R. B. (1991). *Random House Webster's college dictionary*. New York: Random House.

Covey, S. R. (1989). *The 7 habits of highly effective people: Powerful lessons in personal change*. New York: Simon & Schuster.

Dawson, P., & Guare, R. (2009). *Smart but scattered: The revolutionary "executive skills" approach to helping kids reach their full potential*. New York: Guilford Press.

Drew P. v. Clarke County School District, 877 F.2d 927 (11th Cir. 1989).

Florida Department of Education. (2000). *Developing quality individual educational plans: A guide for instructional personnel and families* (rev. ed.). Tallahassee: Florida Department of Education.

Garcia Coll, C., Kagan, J., & Resnick, J. S. (1984). Behavioral inhibition to the unfamiliar. *Child Development*, *55*, 1005–1019.

Gena, A., Krantz, P. J., McClannahan, L. D., & Poulson, C. L. (1996). Training and generalization of affective behavior displayed by youth with autism. *Journal of Applied Behavior Analysis*, *29*(3), 291–304.

Gaylord-Ross, R. J., Haring, T. J., Breen, C., & Pitts-Conway, V. (1984). The training and generalization of social interaction skills with autistic youth. *Journal of Applied Behavior Analysis*, *17*(2), 229–247.

Gillberg, C., & Ehlers, S. (1998). High-functioning people with autism and Asperger syndrome: A literature review. In E. Schopler, G. B. Mesibov, & L. J. Kunce (eds.), *Asperger syndrome or high-functioning autism?* (pp. 79–106). New York: Plenum Press.

Gioia, G. A., Isquith, P. K., Guy, S.C., & Kenworthy, L. (2000). *Behavior rating inventory of executive function*. Odessa, FL: Psychological Assessment Resources.

Goldstein, G., Minshew, N. J., & Siegel, D. J. (1994). Age differences in academic achievement in high-functioning autistic individuals. *Journal of Clinical and Experimental Neuropsychology*, *16*(5), 671–680.

Gray, C. (2010). *The New Social Story™ Book*. Arlington, TX: Future Horizons.

Groden, J., LeVasseur, P., Diller, A., & Cautela, J. (2001). *Coping with stress through picture rehearsal: A how-to manual for working with individuals with autism and developmental disabilities*. Providence, RI: Groden Center.

Hobson, P. (1989). Beyond cognition: A theory of autism. In G. Dawson (ed.), *Autism: Nature, diagnosis, and treatment* (pp. 22–48). New York: Guilford Press.

Ihrig, K., & Wolchik, S. A. (1988). Peer versus adult models and autistic children's learning: Acquisition, generalization, and maintenance. *Journal of Autism and Developmental Disorders*, *18*(1), 49–67.

Klin, A., & Volkmar, F. R. (2000). Treatment and intervention guidelines for individuals with Asperger syndrome. In A. Klin, F. R. Volkmar, & S. S. Sparrow (eds.), *Asperger syndrome* (pp. 340–366). New York: Guilford Press.

Koegel, R. L., Koegel, L. K., & O'Neill, R. (1989). Generalization in the treatment of autism. In L. V. McReynolds & J. E. Sprandlin (eds.), *Generalization strategies in the treatment of communication disorders* (pp. 116–131). Toronto: B. C. Decker.

Landa, R. (2000). Social language use in Asperger syndrome and high-functioning autism. In A. Klin, F. R. Volkmar, & S. S. Sparrow (eds.), *Asperger syndrome* (pp. 125–155). New York: Guilford Press.

Lord, C., Rutter, M., DiLavore, P. C., & Risi, S. (2002). *Autism diagnostic observation schedule*. Los Angeles: Western Psychological Services.

Mager, R. F. (1997a). *Measuring instructional results (or got a match): How to find out if your instructional objectives have been achieved* (3rd ed.). Atlanta: Center for Effective Performance.

Mager, R. F. (1997b). *Preparing instructional objectives: A critical tool in the development of effective instruction* (3rd ed.). Atlanta: Center for Effective Performance.

Mamen, M. (2007). *Understanding nonverbal learning disabilities: A common sense guide for parents and professionals*. London: Jessica Kingsley Publishers.

Minshew, N. J., Goldstein, G., Taylor, H. G., & Siegel, D. J. (1994). Academic achievement in high-functioning autistic individuals. *Journal of Clinical and Experimental Neuropsychology*, *16*(2), 261–270.

Mundy, P., & Sigman, M. (1989). The theoretical implications of joint attention deficits in autism. *Development and Psychopathology*, *1*, 173–183.

Olley, G. J., & Stevenson, S. E. (1989). Preschool curriculum for children with autism: Addressing early social skills. In G. Dawson (ed.), *Autism: Nature, diagnosis, and treatment* (pp. 346–366). New York: Guilford Press.

Ozonoff, S. (1997). Components of executive function in autism and other disorders. In J. Russell (ed.), *Autism as an executive disorder* (pp. 179–211). New York: Oxford University Press.

Peeters, T., & Gillberg, C. (1999). *Autism: Medical and educational aspects* (2nd ed.). London: Whurr.

Pennington, B. F., Bennetto, L., McAleer, O., & Roberts, R. J., Jr. (1996). Executive function and working memory: Theoretical and measurement issues. In G. R. Lyon & N. A. Krasnegor (eds.), *Attention, memory, and executive function* (pp. 327–348). Baltimore: Paul H. Brookes.

Powers, M. D. (1992). Early intervention for children with autism. In D. E. Berkell (ed.), *Autism: Identification, education, and treatment* (pp. 225–252). Hillsdale, NJ: Erlbaum.

Rief, S. F. (2005). *How to reach and teach children with ADD/ADHD: Practical techniques, strategies, and interventions (2nd ed.).* San Francisco: Jossey-Bass.

Rincover, A., & Koegel, R. L. (1975). Setting generality and stimulus control in autistic children. *Journal of Applied Behavior Analysis, 8*, 235–246.

Sevcik, R. A., & Romski, M. A. (1997). Comprehension and language acquisition: Evidence from youth with cognitive disabilities. In L. B. Adamson & M. A. Romski (eds.), *Communication and language acquisition: Discoveries from atypical development* (pp. 187–202). Baltimore: Paul H. Brookes.

Siegel, L. M. (2001). *The complete IEP guide: How to advocate for your special ed child* (2nd ed.). Berkeley: Nolo Press.

Sigman, M., Mundy, P., Sherman, T., & Ungerer, J. (1986). Social interactions of autistic, mentally retarded, and normal children and their caregivers. *Journal of Child Psychology and Psychiatry, 27*, 647–656.

Steedman, W. D. (Summer, 2005). 10 tips for using IDEA 2004 to improve education for children with disabilities. *Autism Spectrum Quarterly*. Higganum, CT: Starfish Specialty Press.

Steedman, W. D. (Fall/Winter, 2005). Tips for using IDEA 2004 to improve education for children with disabilities: An elaboration on tips one through five. *Autism Spectrum Quarterly*. Higganum, CT: Starfish Specialty Press.

Stokes, T. F., & Osnes, P. G. (1988). The developing applied technology of generalization and maintenance. In R. Horner, G. Dunlap, & R. L. Koegel (eds.), *Generalization and maintenance* (pp. 5–19). Baltimore: Paul H. Brookes.

Tager-Flusberg, H., & Sullivan, K. (1994). Predicting and explaining behavior: A comparison of autistic, mentally retarded, and normal children. *Journal of Child Psychology and Psychiatry, 35*(6), 1059–1075.

Tanguay, P. B. (2001). *Nonverbal learning disabilities at home: A parent's guide*. London: Jessica Kingsley Publishers.

Tantum, D. (2000). Adolescence and adulthood in individuals with Asperger syndrome. In A. Klin, F. R. Volkmar, & S. S. Sparrow (eds.), *Asperger syndrome* (pp. 367–399). New York: Guilford Press.

Taylor, B. A., & Harris, S. L. (1995). Teaching children with autism to seek information: Acquisition of novel information and generalization of responding. *Journal of Applied Behavior Analysis, 28*(1), 3–14.

Twachtman-Cullen, D. (1998). Language and communication in high-functioning autism and Asperger syndrome. In E. Schopler, G. B. Mesibov, & L. J. Kunce (eds.), *Asperger syndrome or high-functioning autism?* (pp. 199–225). New York: Plenum Press.

Twachtman-Cullen, D. (2000a). *How to be a para pro: A comprehensive training manual for paraprofessionals*. Higganum, CT: Starfish Specialty Press.

Twachtman-Cullen, D. (2000b). More able children with autism spectrum disorders: Sociocommunicative challenges and guidelines for enhancing abilities. In A. M. Wetherby & B. M. Prizant (eds.), *Autism spectrum disorders: A transactional developmental perspective* (pp. 225–249). Baltimore: Paul H. Brookes.

Twachtman-Cullen, D. (2000c). Asperger syndrome: What we don't know we cannot address. *Journal of Developmental and Learning Disorders*, *4*(1), 83–107.

Twachtman-Cullen, D. (2001, February 23). Paraprofessional support: It's a two-way street. *The Special Educator*, *16*(14), 1, 10.

Twachtman-Cullen, D. (2008). Symbolic communication: Common pathways and points of departure. In K. Dunn Buron & P. Wolfberg (eds.), *Learners on the autism spectrum: Preparing highly qualified educators* (pp. 88–112). Shawnee Mission, KS: Autism Asperger Publishing.

Vygotsky, L. S. (1978). *Mind and society: The development of higher mental process*. Cambridge, MA: Harvard University Press. [Original work published 1930, 1933, and 1935]

Wolfberg, P. (2009). *Play and imagination in children with autism* (2nd ed.). New York: Teachers College Press.

Woods, T. S. (1987). The technology of instruction: A behavior analytic approach. In D. J. Cohen & A. M. Donnellan (eds.), *Handbook of autism and pervasive developmental disorders* (pp. 251–272). New York: Wiley.

Wright, P.W.D., & Wright, P. D. (1999). Wrightslaw: Special education law. Hartfield, VA: Harbor House Law Press.

Wright, P.W.D., & Wright, P. D. (2006). Wrightslaw: Special education law (2nd ed.). Hartfield, VA: Harbor House Law Press.

Wrightslaw. (2010). *Roadmap to IDEA 2004: IEPs, highly qualified teachers, & research based instruction*. http://www.wrightslaw.com/law/idea/ieps.rbi.htm Retrieved June 21, 2010.

INDEX

CPSIA information can be obtained
at www.ICGtesting.com
Printed in the USA
LVHW101923120419
614032LV00009B/47/P

9 780470 562345